COMPARING
SPIRITUALITIES

COMPARING SPIRITUALITIES

FORMATIVE CHRISTIANITY AND JUDAISM ON FINDING LIFE AND MEETING DEATH

**BRUCE CHILTON
AND JACOB NEUSNER**

TRINITY PRESS INTERNATIONAL
HARRISBURG, PENNSYLVANIA

Trinity Press International, P.O. Box 1321, Harrisburg, PA 17105
Trinity Press International is a division of the Morehouse Group.

Cover design by Jim Booth

Library of Congress Cataloging-in-Publication Data

Chilton, Bruce.
    Comparing spiritualities : formative Christianity and Judaism on finding life and meeting death / by Bruce Chilton and Jacob Neusner.
        p. cm.
    Includes bibliographical references and index.
    ISBN 1-56338-309-8 (pbk. : alk paper)
    1. Spiritual life – Judaism. 2. Spiritual life – Christianity.
    3. Judaism – Relations – Christianity. 4. Christianity and other religions – Judaism
    5. Death – Religious aspects – Comparative studies. 6. Martyrdom – Comparative studies.
    I. Neusner, Jacob, 1932–
    BM723.C46 2000
    261.2′6 – dc21   99-057784

Printed in the United States of America

00   01   02   03   04   05   06   10   9   8   7   6   5   4   3   2   1

Contents

Preface

Raising issues of spirituality, this book presents a theological exchange between Judaism, represented by its classical writings, and Christianity, formulated in its initial canon, that of orthodox, catholic Christian tradition. We cover three dimensions of the religious life lived by both religious traditions equally: knowing God, dying in good faith, and bearing faithful witness to God through martyrdom — two of them common human experiences, the third an exemplary one. When we speak of meeting God and of how we die, we take up human experiences that the faithful of Torah and Christ know full well. And, in the aftermath of the Holocaust and in the age in which Christians in Africa and Asia suffer for their faith, we, alas, share knowledge of what the martyr exemplifies for us all. These three dimensions of the inner, spiritual life of faith take the human measure of what it means to live life in the Torah, for Judaism, or in Christ, for Christianity.

In these pages we explore chapters in our shared and common humanity in which, expressing what is distinctive to ourselves, we turn out to speak to the human condition shared with the other. What are experiences both distinctive to the spiritual life of Torah and Christ, respectively, and also accessible to our common humanity? We have chosen the indicated three moments that frame the inner life of faith: birth in the faith, death by the faith, and bearing witness to the faith. The first concerns the encounter with God through the faith's medium of divine self-manifestation. In the instance of Judaism, that means the initial encounter with the Torah, not as a source of information about God, but as the occasion for the meeting with God. In the instance of Christianity, that means permitting the power of God's spirit to bring us to the vision of divine sovereignty, the realization of who we are. The second addresses the fate and destiny of us all, which is death. Here we want to know, how does the pious person die? And what do the faithful of the Torah and of Christ anticipate then? The third turns from the ordinary to the exemplary and asks how the respective traditions define the martyr, the one who gives up life itself to bear witness to the truth of faith.

So we turn to a dialogue concerning what unites us. Christian and Jew, we also are human beings, alike and not alike, but more alike than not. We concur on the centrality of tradition in religious life, so we are alike. The one is a priest, the other a rabbi, so we are not alike. We share the conviction that God desires and hears prayer. But we pray very differently. We concur that God is made manifest to humanity. But we differ on how, when, where, and in what context, in the here and now we meet God. We revere the same Scriptures, which the one knows as the Old Testament, the other as the Written Torah. But we read them differently, the priest looking backward to find Christ in prophecy, the rabbi looking forward to find the Oral Torah in the written part. We have spent many years outlining our differences, undertaking a labor of comparison and contrast. Now has come the time to ask how, *in those very differences*, we meet.

How do experiences that mark us as most distinctive also bring us together? We go in quest for the same God, we proceed toward a common fate, and we value the witness of the exemplary figure of faith. Each finds God, the one in Christ, the other in the Torah. Then the experience of discovery is shared. Comparing the representation of the good death in the two great traditions of the West allows us to write together a single account of dying, in two distinct, but (we think) continuous chapters, the one leading to the other. Both live in preparation for death: how do Christ and the Torah-sage, respectively, embody the model of what that means? And the convictions of both encompass the example of giving life for God's sake, the one on the cross, the other in martyrdom.

These three experiences — discovering life with God, living unto death, and the contemplation of martyrdom — stand each in its own way for the critical moments in the spiritual life of Christ and the Torah. We accordingly propose to portray the way in which the classical statements of Christ and the Torah represent critical moments in a person's life of faith and to compare the spirituality, the piety, that each of the two religions of Israel's Scriptures means to nurture. The comparison, yielding commonalities, finds its justification in a single, simple fact: at the concrete moment of encounter with God, the religions of Christ and of the Torah agree that they meet one and the same God, the God made known to Israel in Scripture, prophecy, and tradition. That comparison is the charge of monotheism set forth in a jointly held Scripture.

Where and how in the encounter with the shared human condition the one's Christ (that is to say, Christianity) and the other's Torah (that is to say, Judaism) teach us how to live and die defines the issue of this book. Interfaith dialogue in the English-speaking world has brought to an end both Judaic isolationism and Christian imperialism. But, from where we now stand, we know the whence that has ended, but not the whither that beckons. Both the great traditions of the same Scriptures of ancient Israel, Christianity and Judaism, pray for eschatological reconciliation, when (in the language of Judaism) all humanity will acknowledge the unity of God, or (in the language of Christianity) all believers shall be one as the Father and the Son are one. But in prayer each asks God to bring the other home, the rabbi to the one God made manifest in the Torah, the priest to Christ, respectively. So if the end of days does not serve to define the path we seek, what does? Our answer is, our common stake in chapters of human existence that encompass us both.

At issue here, then, is whether and how the Torah and Christ speak to the same humanity, engaged in the conduct of lives of a common quality. Judaism and Christianity speak of living life under God, one God, the only God, the same God for us all. We give testimony to a God that is sovereign and good. We share fundamental assumptions, such as, in the words of Walter Moberly:

> The dignity of human life, the centrality of love, trust, obedience, mercy, forgiveness; the living of the life of faith in community; prayer as the essential medium between God and humanity.[1]

We can respond to the poetry of the other, the yearning for God conveyed by the other, the love of God that nourishes the other. Toward a Judaeo-Christian dialogue of quest, each for a tale to tell the authentic humanity of the other, events of this awful past century have brought us.

Clearly, we have chosen to privilege, among all religions, the relationship and dialogue between Christianity and Judaism. That is not a happenstance. We regard that relationship as unique, no other two religions replicating anything remotely similar to the intimacy between the two religions of the Judaeo-Christian West. Why, among all religions accessible through their writings, compare the spirituality of Christianity and Judaism in particular? If Christianity were wholly unlike Judaism, then any dialogue with Christianity on the part of Judaism would begin with the recognition that the other is wholly other: beyond all parallels, comparisons and contrasts. And if Judaism were totally out of relationship to Christianity, then any dialogue with Judaism on the part

---

1. Personal letter, August 8, 1991.

of Christianity would also commence with the understanding that the Christian stood utterly out of relationship with Judaism.

But, we maintain — and in a variety of works we believe we have demonstrated — that the categorical structures of the two religions correspond to one another. That is because Judaism and Christianity rest upon a single, shared conviction: God is one, unique, but known to humanity through the prophets of ancient Israel, beginning with the patriarchs and extending through Moses at Sinai. However, not theology but existential encounter defines the issue of this book: How, in turning to God, do we remain accessible to the other? In what ways does the common experience of death unite us? And how do the martyrs of our respective faiths turn out to exemplify a virtue each of us may find in the other?

Given the diversity characteristic of the families of kindred religious traditions formed by Judaism and by Christianity, respectively, we have to specify what we mean in these pages by "Judaism" and by "Christianity." The answer in both instances is the classical writings to which the generality of Judaic and Christian religious systems, over time, respectively refer. We focus on the classical and definitive documents of the two traditions. Because the sources on which we dwell endure as the heritage for Judaisms and Christianities over time, we represent them as the starting point for any picture of the spirituality and piety of the two faiths — the starting point, not the final word.

For Judaism that is the Torah as it took shape in the first six centuries of the Common Era (=A.D.) for revelation; the account of who and what is "Israel" in those same writings; the exposition of ways in which, in everyday life, God enters into the situation of ordinary people — how we meet God this morning, right here, as those documents portray the encounter. Which documents? Like Christianity, Judaism begins in the writings of ancient Israel and appeals to the Hebrew Scriptures that the world knows as "the Old Testament" and that Judaism calls "the written Torah." But Judaism appeals also to oral traditions called "the Oral Torah." So, like Christianity, Judaism values additional writings. To state the matter in simple language: The New Testament is to the Old Testament as the Oral Torah is to the Written Torah.

What is the meaning of this keyword, "Torah"? The word covers a number of matters. "The Torah" refers first of all to the Pentateuch, the Five Books of Moses: Genesis, Exodus, Leviticus, Numbers, and Deuteronomy. These are inscribed in a scroll, read aloud in synagogue worship, carefully protected as a holy object — "the Torah." So by "the

Torah" Judaism means the object, the holy scroll that sets forth the Pentateuch. But the Torah comprises, further, the remainder of the Hebrew Scriptures, the Prophets and the Writings. The Prophets are the books of Joshua, Judges, Samuel, Kings, Isaiah, Jeremiah, and Ezekiel, as well as the twelve smaller collections. The Writings encompass Psalms, Proverbs, Chronicles, Job, the Five Scrolls (Lamentations, Esther, Ruth, Song of Songs, a.k.a. Song of Solomon, and Qoheleth, a.k.a. Ecclesiastes). All together, if we take the first letters of the three words, Torah, Nebi'im, and Ketubim, the Torah (Pentateuch), Prophets (Hebrew: Nebi'im), and Writings (Hebrew: Ketubim) yield the Hebrew neologism for the Old Testament, TaNaKH.

But since Judaism, like Christianity, values further traditions as divinely revealed at Sinai, by "the Torah" more writings are encompassed. Specifically, classical Judaism, which took shape in the first seven centuries of the Common Era (c.e.), by "the Oral Torah" means traditions revealed by God to Moses at Sinai — oral traditions right along with the written Torah (Genesis through Deuteronomy). These other traditions were preserved orally, in a process of oral formulation and oral transmission, from Sinai through prophets and elders, masters and disciples, until they were finally reduced to written form in a set of documents that reached closure from ca. 200 to ca. 600 c.e. All together, these documents are classified as "the Oral Torah," meaning the repositories of the oral tradition of Sinai.

What are the documents that initially comprise "the Oral Torah"? The first and most important of them is the Mishnah, a law code of a deeply philosophical character, closed at 200 c.e.. The code quickly attracted commentators, who analyzed its contents and clarified and applied its rules. The work of the commentators was put together and written down. It reaches us in two Talmuds, that is, two distinct traditions of explanation of the Mishnah: the Talmud of the Land of Israel, which reached a conclusion at ca. 400 c.e. in what was then Roman-ruled Palestine, and the Talmud of Babylonia, finished at ca. 600 c.e. in Iranian-ruled Babylonia (approximately the area of central Iraq today).

Once the work of explaining the Mishnah got underway, the same approaches to the reading of the received tradition led the Judaic sages to provide the Hebrew Scriptures with compilations setting forth extensive explanation and amplification. This work of rereading Scripture in light of contemporary questions was called "Midrash," from the Hebrew word, "darash," meaning "search." In the formative age of the Judaism based on the written and the oral traditions of Sinai, a number of compilations of readings of scriptural books were completed. In particular, books of the written Torah that are read in synagogue services received systematic exposition. To the book of Genesis was attached Genesis Rabbah (the amplification of Genesis); so, too, to Leviticus, Leviticus Rabbah; to Exodus came a work amplifying the normative rules of Exodus, called Mekhilta attributed to R. Ishmael; to Leviticus another legal commentary, Sifra; to Numbers and Deuteronomy legal commentaries called Sifré to Numbers and Sifré to Deuteronomy. Four of the Five Scrolls (Ruth, Esther, Song of Songs, and Lamentations) were systematically reread. In medieval times, other compilations addressed the books of the Written Torah neglected in the formative age.

For Christianity, the counterpart categories address engaging with God through Christ, his reign of forceful grace, and Christ as the bodily presence of God on earth. Christian faith understands itself to be grounded in the Holy Spirit, God's communication of himself. Access to the Holy Spirit is possible because in Jesus Christ God became human. The Incarnation (God becoming flesh, *caro* in Latin) is what provides the possibility of divine Spirit becoming accessible to the human spirit.

Speaking from the perspective of Christian faith, then, there is a single source of theology: the Holy Spirit which comes from the Father and Son. But the inspiration of the Holy Spirit has been discovered and articulated by means of distinct kinds of literature in the history of the Church. By becoming aware of the diversity of those sources, both the variety and the coherence of Christianity may be appreciated.

The Scriptures of Israel have always been valued within the Church, both in Hebrew and in the Greek translation used in the Mediterranean world. (The Greek rendering is called the "Septuagint," after the seventy translators who were said to have produced it.) Those were the only Scriptures of the Church in its primitive phase, when the New Testament was being composed. In their meetings of prayer and worship, followers of Jesus saw the Scriptures of Israel "fulfilled" by their faith: their conviction was that the same Spirit of God which was active in the prophets was, through Christ, available to them.

The New Testament was produced in primitive communities of Christians to prepare people for baptism, to order worship, to resolve disputes, to encourage faith, and to accomplish like purposes. As a whole, it is a collective document of primitive Christianity. Its purpose is to call out and order true Israel in response to the triumphant news of Jesus' preaching, activity, death, and resurrection. The New Testament provides the means of accessing the Spirit spoken of in the Scriptures of Israel. Once the New Testament was formed, it was natural to refer to the Scriptures of Israel as the "Old Testament."

The Old Testament is classic for Christians because it represents the ways in which God's Spirit might be known. At the same time, the New Testament is normative: it sets out how we actually appropriate the Spirit of God, which is also the spirit of Christ. That is why the Bible as a whole is accorded a place of absolute privilege in the Christian tradition: it is the literary source from which we know both how the Spirit of God has been known and how we can appropriate it.

Early Christianity (between the second and the fourth centuries c.e.) designates the period during which the Church founded theology on the basis of the Scriptures. Although Christians were under extreme — sometimes violent — pressure from the Roman Empire, Early Christianity was a time of unique creativity. From thinkers as different from one another as Bishop Irenaeus in France and as Origen, the speculative teacher active first in Egypt and then in Palestine, a commonly Christian philosophy began to emerge. Early Christianity might also be called a "Catholic" faith, in the sense that it was a quest for a "general" or "universal" account of the phase, but that designation may lead to confusion with Roman Catholicism at a later stage and is avoided here.

After the Roman Empire itself embraced Christianity in the fourth century, the Church was in a position formally to articulate its understanding of the faith by means of common standards. During this period of Orthodox Christianity, correct norms of worship, baptism, creeds, biblical texts, and doctrines were established. From Augustine in the West to Gregory of Nyssa in the East, Christianity for the first and only time in its history approached being truly ecumenical.

Both authors elect to limit discussion to the classical, normative writings, in the clear recognition that both religions unfolded through time, so that later writers expanded and recast the classical definitions and even categories. But we maintain that, however through time things changed, the classical formulation remains the paramount one, the touchstone of other developments.

Why do we think the comparison of spiritualities, Christian and Judaic, in quest of a shared human experience, is worth undertaking? Both have known one God, whether in the person of Jesus Christ, God incarnate, or in the revelation of the one whole Torah given by God to Moses at Sinai. But believing in one and the same God, appealing to one and the same story of creation, sharing prophets in common, such as Abraham and Moses, Jeremiah and Isaiah, and referring to revelation, shared (from Sinai and the prophets) like children of common parents, they have sustained for most of their lives on earth a certain loathing on the one side, and an utter incapacity to communicate, on the other. So they have turned inward, each religion talking to its own audience, none proposing to speak beyond its own walls, except to explain to the others how misguided about God they are. At best each offered the outsiders tolerance, bestowed perforce; often, a malign relativism — declaring each is right for its own — masks mutual incomprehension.

Whether even now one religion wishes to talk with another is not altogether clear. But that the world will listen is beyond doubt. For the time to talk has come, when each party has gained something of what it has long wanted: Christianity no longer beset in Europe itself by a well-entrenched and strong alternative in Communism, Judaism no longer bereft of place, a social order for which it states the norm. So they can look beyond themselves. But for what? Judaism on its own makes no sense of Jesus Christ, God incarnate, in terms Christians can recognize as authentic to their faith; Christianity, on its own, cannot grasp Israel, God's first love, in terms holy Israel can comprehend. Election and Incarnation, keystones of the faith of Judaism and Christianity, respectively, will stand for mutual hatred unless they are mutually understood. So if the moment presents its opportunity, it can only be to accomplish what at no prior hour, in no earlier circumstance, the faiths of the one God — known through Abraham, the Torah, Christ, respectively — have achieved.

And that is not so grand a thing as making sense of difference, understanding how one and the same God whom all of us worship and love and serve could have said so many contradictory things to those to whom, through Christ and Torah respectively, that one true God addressed humanity: Church, Israel. Perhaps another age will work its way toward that deep question, beyond our searching out. For us, a great step forward will be the simple journey toward understanding: the possibility, even, of conversation, each in his own idiom, about experiences both know or will know or can know. For a long time, perhaps for all time, we have not conversed at all. The times are such that the time has come to talk. The first step clearly leads Judaism to undertake dialogue with Christianity, and Christianity with Judaism. We think that conversation about what we know, each in his own way, about an experience that we share marks a good starting point.

The present work carries forward the authors' shared project of laying foundations for interfaith dialogue among Judaic and Christian faithful, a dialogue of intellectual, theological substance, not political formality or essentially secular social meliorism. Before turning, here, to comparing spiritualities, we have worked in the areas of historical, literary and philosophical, and theological comparison.

Both authors hold professorships at Bard College, Mr. Chilton as Bernard Iddings Bell Professor of Religion and Philosophy, and Mr. Neusner as Research Professor of Religion and Theology. Bard provides a happy meeting place for their ongoing scholarly dialogue and continuing partnership in undergraduate teaching as well. In addition, Mr. Neusner is Distinguished Research Professor of Religious Studies at the University of South Florida, Tampa. Both Bard and USF provide generous research grants, and Mr. Chilton has enjoyed the support of the Pew Charitable Trusts (Evangelical Scholars Program), for which thanks are given.

BRUCE CHILTON
JACOB NEUSNER

ONE

Discovering the Torah

Rabban Yohanan ben Zakkai would say, "If you have learned much Torah, do not puff yourself up on that account, for it was for that purpose that you were created. For people were created only on the stipulation that they should occupy themselves with the Torah."
— THE FATHERS ACCORDING TO RABBI NATHAN XIV:II.1

Why does Yohanan ben Zakkai maintain that it was to study the Torah that humanity was created? It is because, in his view, as in the view of Judaism in its classical statement, God is made manifest in the Torah and only there. People reasonably think otherwise, finding God in the stars or in ourselves, in the power of the seas or in the silence of the desert. But unless God tells us that there God is, we do not know it. God is not made manifest in nature, outside of the Torah's account of natural creation. Nor is God made known through what happens in history, outside of the Torah's interpretation of events. That is to say, if the Torah did not tell us that the heavens tell the glory of God, how should we know? And if the Torah did not tell us that Assyria was the rod of God's wrath, how might we have come to such a conclusion? Without the Torah, nature and history fall dumb — or set forth messages too diverse to command universal assent. And, it goes without saying but has always to be repeated, Israel receives the Torah in community. There is no revelation to Israel that does not take place in the Torah or in entire unity with the Torah. The mountains danced — for Israel at Sinai. The kings heard the roar — of God at Sinai. Nature and politics or history find their sense — through God at Sinai, in this morning's giving of the Torah.

Holy Israel meets God in the Torah, which is God's self-manifestation to Israel and humanity. Holy Israel assembles to study the Torah in two places: synagogue and yeshiva or center for the study of Torah for God's sake. It follows that the conduct of holy Israel in the synagogue and academy or yeshiva in the hour of the giving and the receiving of the

Torah marks the moment and the locus at which Israel meets God. In the words and music, gesture and movement, dance and drama and sentiment, attitude, and emotion of that moment, God is made manifest in the congregation of Israel. That is where God has chosen to become known to humanity — so the Torah says, so holy Israel affirms. What Israel finds in the Torah is knowledge of God, the record of God's love of humanity, and the details of that record in good faith. The faith of the Torah is coherent, proportioned, cogent, logical, and rational, within the framework of its premises and its established truths and its givens and its facts. The Torah properly studied tells us about God: where and how we know God. And when it comes to studying the Torah, the right word for describing the discovery of what is at issue is "turning," as in the Hebrew, "repentance," for Torah-study is a turning to God. When we tell the stories of how sages discovered the Torah and undertook to study it, we deal with the moment of what in Western languages we call "conversion."

And that fact calls to mind the single most famous event of conversion in Western history. When, preoccupied with the followers of Jesus, Saul took the road to Damascus, he met the risen Christ and so found the reason for his life. Paul's contemporary, Yohanan ben Zakkai, in the saying cited at the head of this chapter identifies a different focus for life, which is study of the Torah. That is because, in Judaism, Torah-study sets the occasion on which the faithful meet God. In the holy community of Israel they find God in the Torah, through studying the Torah, meaning not only Scripture ("the Old Testament," "the Written Torah") but the Oral part of the Torah as well, formulated orally and handed on by memory from Sinai, only to be written down long afterward in the documents of the ancient rabbis of the first six centuries C.E. Because it was in writing, anyone could gain access to the Written part of the Torah. But because it was handed on orally, through memorization, from master to disciple, only disciples of masters could enter into the disciplines of the Oral Torah. Then Judaism will identify in the moment that an Israelite determines to study the Torah the counterpart to the event on the road to Damascus. In the classical statement of Judaism, Torah-study is where and how Israel meets God.

That is for two reasons. First of all, it is in the Torah that the record of God's self-manifestation and revelation to Israel is conveyed; what holy Israel knows about God it learns in that record. Sages would claim in behalf of that record — the whole Torah, oral and written — two traits. First of all, the Torah reveals God's will for Israel; second, the Torah is both authoritative and open-ended. The former represents a negative, the latter a positive, charge. The Torah is authoritative in that all other claims to reveal God's will come under the judgment of the Torah, oral and written, and those inconsistent with the Torah cannot stand. But on the positive side, the Torah also is open-ended in that those sages and disciples who master the principles of the Torah, its rules of thought, analysis, argument, and decision-making, themselves participate in the revelation at Sinai. The Torah reveals, above all, God's words in God's own formulation, and through the close and thoughtful study of those words, humanity can enter into God's way of thinking, into the mind of God. Those who today read nature as a picture of the Creator's intellect and plan will understand the sages' conviction that reading the Torah as God's self-revelation leads the disciple directly into the intellect of the One who revealed the Torah: his words, in his way of formulating his will.

These convictions of the classical statement of Judaism explain why Torah-study makes such a difference as to warrant comparison, as to spirituality, with the moment of encounter and conversion in the analogy of Paul's meeting on the road to Damascus. It is because through what he masters in the Torah, the Israelite meets God. And what is at stake is not personal — the conversion of the individual, the salvation of the soul of a private person. On the contrary, meeting God in the Torah, the sage brings God's presence to rest upon Israel. This is expressed in the following way:

A. "And it came to pass in the days of Ahaz" (Isa. 7:1).

B. What was the misfortune that took place at that time?

C. "The Syrians on the east and the Philistines on the west [devour Israel with open mouth]" (Isa. 9:12).

D. The matter [the position of Israel] may be compared to a king who handed over his son to a tutor, who hated [the son]. The tutor thought, "If I kill him now, I shall turn out to be liable to the death penalty before the king. So what I'll do is take away his wet nurse, and he will die on his own."

E. So thought Ahaz, "If there are no kids, there will be no he-goats. If there are no he-goats, there will be no flock. If there is no flock, there will be no shepherd. If there is no shepherd, there will be no world."

F. So did Ahaz plan, "If there are no children, there will be no disciples; if there are no disciples, there will be no sages; if there are
no sages, there will be no Torah; if there is no Torah, there will be
no synagogues and schools; if there are no synagogues and schools,
then the Holy One, blessed be he, will not allow his Presence to
come to rest in the world."

G. What did he do? He went and locked the synagogues and schools.
— LEVITICUS RABBAH XI:VII.3

The base verse, Isa. 7:1, is understood to refer to a misfortune, and the
misfortune was that Israel was surrounded on the east and the west. This
is then translated into a plan to annihilate Israel that Ahaz formulated,
the plan to destroy Israel by denying Israel access to God through the
Torah. How does this take place? He will kill the children and close
the schools. That will turn off the flow of disciples. There will then be
no masters, sages of the Torah, and that will remove the Torah from
Israel. The synagogues and schools will close. But it is to the synagogues
and the schools that God's presence comes to Israel. So, to shortcut the
process, Ahaz locked the doors of the synagogues and schools — and the
Holy Spirit was locked out of Israel. Framing the matter in simple terms:
Through the Torah God comes into the world, and the sages, who master
the Torah and teach it, therefore bring God into the world.

Note the difference between Saul, by himself, meeting Christ all alone,
and the encounter with God through God's presence in schoolhouses and
synagogues. While the Torah may be studied in private, it is received
and proclaimed only in the public square of shared worship or shared
learning: synagogue, yeshiva. One's obligation to hear the Torah read
can be fulfilled only in community, in a quorum. That is where we meet
God. This is the point of Rabbi Halafta of Kefar Hananiah, in a familiar
saying of Torah-learning that explains how we meet God in the Torah:

"Among ten who sit and work hard on Torah the Presence comes
to rest, as it is said, 'God stands in the congregation of God' (Ps.
82:1). And how do we know that the same is so even of five? For
it is said, 'And he has founded his group upon the earth' (Amos
9:6). And how do we know that this is so even of three? Since it is
said, 'And he judges among the judges' (Ps. 82:1). And how do we
know that this is so even of two? Because it is said, 'Then they that
feared the Lord spoke with one another, and the Lord hearkened
and heard' (Mal. 3:16). And how do we know that this is so even

of one? Since it is said, 'In every place where I record my name I will come to you and I will bless you' (Exod. 20:24)."

— TRACTATE ABOT 3:6

So — Halafta maintains — Israel meets God in the Torah, and that encounter may take place among many or even one on One. But while Halafta has spoken of even a single individual, and, it is manifest, Israel is made up of individuals, still, the Torah is best studied in community, whether palpable, as in a school, or imagined, as in books, articles, or debates in letters.

Israel encounters God together in the Torah through processes of rational thought: systematic description, critical analysis, rational interpretation. To discover the Torah requires finding a community formed around the Torah, oral and written. Why should this be so? By analogy to contemporary science, for the same reason that scholars work together on problems in shared laboratories or in seminars, conferences, meetings. It is to test results and their meaning. The contemporary philosophical — somewhat clunky — words, "universalizability" and "generalizability," serve as the model. These refer to what can be shown to others to be true and can be demonstrated to apply to many cases. Where thought cannot be communicated by some protocol of rationality or convention of agreed signals that sustain communication, we deal with what is not asocial but insane. Rationality is always public, by definition. And, given the public character of the giving of the Torah, the propositional character of what is given, and the active and engaged character of the act of receiving the Torah, it is no surprise that the rule for studying the Torah and therefore also the requirement for meeting God is as with Moses and Elijah. God gives the Torah through the prophet to be sure, but always to the "us" of Israel. So "we" meeting the One may be embodied in the "I," the individual of whom Halafta speaks, but "we" always stands for the "we" of Israel. Rationality requires community.

Does that mean that Israel meets God only in the schoolhouse and in the synagogue, that finding God requires encountering the Torah? The sages themselves tell stories that say the opposite. Sages themselves paint yet another, and conflicting, picture of the extraordinarily virtuous person. They have the notion that the most ignorant of ignorant persons, who devote their lives to sin, can through a single action accomplish what a life devoted to Torah-study cannot achieve. And that brings us back to what transcends Torah-study even in the teaching of the masters of the Torah: the merit of the act of selfless love, the act God cannot compel

or coerce but craves of humanity. The commandment to love God —
"You shall love the Lord your God with all your heart, your soul, and
your might" (Deut. 4:9) — and to love the other — "You shall love your
neighbor as yourself" (Lev. 19:18) — meet and form a single statement.
It is that to which God aspires for us, but what God cannot impose upon
us. God can command love but not coerce it, favor but not force it.
But then God responds to the act of selfless generosity with an act of
grace — precisely that act that humanity for its part cannot compel or
coerce out of God, cannot cajole from God, but can only beseech. In this
story, a humble, ignorant man can accomplish what the rabbis cannot,
and they want to know why.

> L. A certain ass driver appeared before the rabbis [the context re-
> quires: in a dream] and prayed, and rain came. The rabbis sent
> and brought him and said to him, "What is your trade?"

> M. He said to them, "I am an ass driver."

> N. They said to him, "And how do you conduct your business?"

> O. He said to them, "One time I rented my ass to a certain woman,
> and she was weeping on the way, and I said to her, 'What's with
> you?' and she said to me, 'The husband of that woman [me] is in
> prison [for debt], and I wanted to see what I can do to free him.' So
> I sold my ass and I gave her the proceeds, and I said to her, 'Here
> is your money, free your husband, but do not sin [by becoming a
> prostitute to raise the necessary funds].'"

> P. They said to him, "You are worthy of praying and having your
> prayers answered."

> — YERUSHALMI TAANIT 1:4.1

Obviously not a master of Torah-learning, the ass driver clearly has a
powerful lien on Heaven, so that his prayers are answered, even while
those of others are not. What did he do to get that entitlement? He did
what no law could demand: impoverished himself to save the woman
from a "fate worse than death." A more complex body of meritorious
actions is set forth in the following story, which captures the entire range
of virtues that sages valued:

> V. A pious man from Kefar Imi appeared [in a dream] to the rabbis.
> He prayed for rain and it rained. The rabbis went up to him. His
> householders told them that he was sitting on a hill. They went out
> to him, saying to him, "Greetings," but he did not answer them.

W. He was sitting and eating, and he did not say to them, "You break bread too."

X. When he went back home, he made a bundle of faggots and put his cloak on top of the bundle [instead of on his shoulder].

Y. When he came home, he said to his household [wife], "These rabbis are here [because] they want me to pray for rain. If I pray and it rains, it is a disgrace for them, and if not, it is a profanation of the Name of Heaven. But come, you and I will go up [to the roof] and pray. If it rains, we shall tell them, 'We are not worthy to pray and have our prayers answered.'"

Z. They went up and prayed and it rained.

AA. They came down to them [and asked], "Why have the rabbis troubled themselves to come here today?"

BB. They said to him, "We wanted you to pray so that it would rain."

CC. He said to them, "Now do you really need my prayers? Heaven already has done its miracle."

DD. They said to him, "Why, when you were on the hill, did we say hello to you, and you did not reply?"

EE. He said to them, "I was then doing my job. Should I then interrupt my concentration [on my work]?"

FF. They said to him, "And why, when you sat down to eat, did you not say to us 'You break bread too'?"

GG. He said to them, "Because I had only my small ration of bread. Why would I have invited you to eat by way of mere flattery [when I knew I could not give you anything at all]?"

HH. They said to him, "And why, when you came to go down, did you put your cloak on top of the bundle?"

II. He said to them, "Because the cloak was not mine. It was borrowed for use at prayer. I did not want to tear it."

JJ. They said to him, "And why, when you were on the hill, did your wife wear dirty clothes, but when you came down from the mountain, did she put on clean clothes?"

KK. He said to them, "When I was on the hill, she put on dirty clothes, so that no one would gaze at her. But when I came home from the hill, she put on clean clothes, so that I would not gaze on any other woman."

LL. They said to him, "It is well that you pray and have your prayers answered."

— Yerushalmi Taanit 1:4.1

The pious man finally enjoys the recognition of the sages by reason of his lien upon Heaven, able as he is to pray and bring rain. What has so endowed him are his acts of punctiliousness of a moral order: concentrating on his work, avoiding an act of dissimulation, integrity in the disposition of a borrowed object, his wife's concern not to attract other men and her equal concern to make herself attractive to her husband. These stories then tell us about what it means to enjoy not an entitlement by inheritance but a lien accomplished by one's own supererogatory acts of restraint. Torah-learning does not figure in them, and sages explicitly confess that they do not enjoy the signs of God's favor and grace that the heroes of these stories do.

In sages' accounts of matters, such a remarkable action of selfless love, done once, not only makes up for a dissolute life but, in that single moment, wins Heaven's perpetual favor, and, once more, not coerced, God loves the one who without coercion gives love. That person loves and serves God, even without knowing it, clearly without knowledge of the Torah meant to teach what it means to love God freely and without expectation of reward, which is what it means to love God with all one's heart, with all one's soul, and with all one's might:

Q. In a dream of R. Abbahu, Mr. Pentakaka ["Five sins"] appeared, who prayed that rain would come, and it rained. R. Abbahu sent and summoned him. He said to him, "What is your trade?"

R. He said to him, "Five sins does that man [I] do every day, [for I am a pimp:] [1] hiring whores, [2] cleaning up the theater, [3] bringing home their garments for washing, [4] dancing, and [5] 'performing' before them."

S. He said to him, "And what sort of decent thing have you ever done?"

T. He said to him, "One day that man [I] was cleaning the theater, and a woman came and stood behind a pillar and cried. I said to her, 'What's with you?' And she said to me, 'That woman's [my] husband is in prison, and I wanted to see what I can do to free him,' so I sold my bed and cover, and I gave the proceeds to her. I said to her, 'Here is your money, free your husband, but do not sin.'"

U. He said to him, "You are worthy of praying and having your prayers answered."

— YERUSHALMI TAANIT 1:4.1

Mr. Five-Sins has done everything sinful that (within sages' imagination) one can do, and, more to the point, he does it every day. What he should do is carry out the commandments, and he should study the Torah every day. So what he has done is what he should not have done, and what he has not done is what he should have done — every day. And yet in a single action, in a moment, everything changes. The act at hand forms the mirror-image and opposite of sin. Here again, the single act of saving a woman from a "fate worse than death" has sufficed. Mr. Five-Sins has carried out an act of grace, to which Heaven, uncoerced and uncompelled, responds with that love in which God so richly abounds for humanity. The extraordinary person is the one who sacrifices for the other in an act of selfless love — and that can be anybody, at any time, anywhere.

Nonetheless, when it comes to explaining how Israel meets God, sages tell stories that bear comparison to Paul's account of his encounter on the road to Damascus. But by this point, we now realize, the counterpart will bear these traits: It will be both individual and public. It will involve Torah-study. And, in the nature of things, it will involve the recognition of ignorance and the quest for Torah-learning. So that to which the Israelite within Judaism turns ("converts") is Torah, and the place to which he turns is the schoolhouse. That is why a type of story told about some of the memorable sages will relate how they came to study the Torah, and one of the conventions of that story will stress the ignorance of the mature man, on the one side, and his recognition of that ignorance, on the other. Then the heart of the matter is the realization, the recognition of one's ignorance — and the decision to seek knowledge at all costs:

VI:VI.1

A. How did R. Eliezer ben Hyrcanus begin [his Torah-study]?

B. He had reached the age of twenty-two years and had not yet studied the Torah. One time he said, "I shall go and study the Torah before Rabban Yohanan ben Zakkai."

C. His father Hyrcanus said to him, "You are not going to taste a bit of food until you have ploughed the entire furrow."

D. He got up in the morning and ploughed the entire furrow.

Like conversion experiences in general, this one is sudden, but very specific. Eliezer originates as an unlettered farmer, but, for reasons we do not know, has heard of, and wishes to study Torah with, the greatest figure of his generation, Yohanan ben Zakkai in Jerusalem. But Eliezer keeps the Torah even now: he honors his father and obeys his order.

Now comes the account of how Eliezer accepted penury, even near-starvation, to devote his life to Torah-study. The starvation produced bad breath, which became the basis for a blessing for the deprived disciple:

E. They say that that day was Friday. He went and took a meal with his father in law.

F. And some say that he tasted nothing from the sixth hour on Friday until the sixth hour on Sunday.

VI:VI.2

A. On the way he saw a rock. He picked it up and took it and put it into his mouth.

B. And some say that what he picked up was cattle dung.

C. He went and spent the night at his hostel.

VI:VI.3

A. He went and entered study-session before Rabban Yohanan ben Zakkai in Jerusalem.

B. Since a bad odor came out of his mouth, Rabban Yohanan ben Zakkai said to him, "Eliezer my son, have you taken a meal today?"

C. He shut up.

D. He asked him again, and he shut up again.

E. He sent word and inquired at his hostel, and asked, "Has Eliezer eaten anything with you?"

F. They sent word to him, "We thought that he might be eating with my lord."

G. He said, "For my part, I thought that he might be eating with you. Between me and you, we should have lost R. Eliezer in the middle."

H. He said to him, "Just as the odor of your mouth has gone forth, so will a good name in the Torah go forth for you."

We have seen how the encounter with God is public, communal, not personal and individual. Hence the picture of how the great sage began in mature years, in a situation of ignorance, encompasses the matter of the impact of a turning to Torah-study upon the family of the new disciple of sages. Hyrcanus, Eliezer's father, determined to disinherit his son for leaving the family for the academy. He makes a trip to Jerusalem to impose on Eliezer the vow not to derive benefit from his property:

VI:VI.4

A. Hyrcanus, his father, heard that he was studying the Torah with Rabban Yohanan ben Zakkai. He decided, "I shall go and impose on Eliezer my son a vow not to derive benefit from my property."

Yohanan will now make certain that Hyrcanus sees, close up, the glory that his son has attained in Torah-study:

B. They say that that day Rabban Yohanan ben Zakkai was in session and expounding [the Torah] in Jerusalem, and all the great men of Israel were in session before him. He heard that he was coming. He set up guards, saying to them, "If he comes to take a seat, do not let him."

C. He came to take a seat and they did not let him.

D. He kept stepping over people and moving forward until he came to Ben Sisit Hakkesset and Naqdimon b. Gurion and Ben Kalba Sabua. He sat among them, trembling.

E. They say, On that day Rabban Yohanan ben Zakkai looked at R. Eliezer, indicating to him, "Cite an appropriate passage and give an exposition."

F. He said to him, "I cannot cite an appropriate passage."

G. He urged him, and the other disciples urged him.

H. He went and cited an opening passage and expounded matters the like of which no ear had ever heard.

I. And at every word that he said, Rabban Yohanan ben Zakkai arose and kissed him on his head and said, "My lord, Eliezer, my lord, you have taught us truth."

J. As the time came to break up, Hyrcanus his father stood up and said, "My lords, I came here only to impose a vow on my son, Eliezer, not to derive benefit from my possession. Now all of my possessions are given over to Eliezer my son, and all my other sons are disinherited and will have no share in them."

— The Fathers according to Rabbi Nathan vi:vi

Other versions of the story have Eliezer decline the brothers' share. That is not the point. The point is, the great master of the future has entered a new, supernatural family, even while retaining his ties to his natural family. The contrast with the situation of Saul become Paul cannot be missed. Paul's turning to the risen Christ does not affect his family, of which he says nothing. It is a personal and individual matter, with heavy consequence for the Christian communities that he shapes, but with little result for his standing within the social order of which he is a part.

But that is not the entire story. For just as Jesus identified as his family those who followed him and accepted his message, so sages explicitly identify a supernatural family for the disciple of the sage. For the Torah revealed by God to Moses and handed on by tradition to the very sages of the Mishnah, Midrash, and Talmuds, radically revises all this-worldly relationships and patterns. The Torah sees the natural world from a supernatural perspective, through God's spectacles, so to speak. Accordingly, when it comes to relationships of children to parents — and by extension, all other relationships — the Torah recasts matters in a radical manner.

Specifically, the Torah creates a supernatural family that overtakes the this-worldly family and takes priority over it. That is stated in so many words, when the law specifies that the obligations that a disciple owes to his master transcend those that the son owes to his father:

A. [If he has to choose between seeking] what he has lost and what his father has lost,

B. his own takes precedence.

C. what he has lost and what his master has lost,

D. his own takes precedence.

E. what his father has lost and what his master has lost,

F. that of his master takes precedence.

G. For his father brought him into this world.

H. But his master, who taught him wisdom, will bring him into life.

I. But if his father is a sage, that of his father takes precedence.

J. [If] his father and his master were carrying heavy burdens, he removes that of his master, and afterward removes that of his father.

K. [If] his father and his master were taken captive,

L. he ransoms his master, and afterward he ransoms his father.

M. But if his father is a sage, he ransoms his father, and afterward he ransoms his master.

       — Mishnah-tractate Baba Mesia 2:11

Matters are carried a step further. Holy Israel in its classical law is organized into castes, the highest being the priests, then the Levites, then the Israelites, and so on down. But a disciple of a sage, one in the lowest caste, takes priority over a high priest who has not mastered the Torah. So the family only exemplifies the Torah's deepest ordering of the social relationships of holy Israel, whether in the home or in the public piazza or in the Temple itself:

3:6

A. Whatever is offered more regularly than its fellow takes precedence over its fellow, and whatever is more holy than its fellow takes precedence over its fellow.

B. [If] a bullock of an anointed priest and a bullock of the congregation [M. Hor. 1:5] are standing [awaiting sacrifice] —

C. the bullock of the anointed [high priest] takes precedence over the bullock of the congregation in all rites pertaining to it.

3:7

A. The man takes precedence over the woman in the matter of the saving of life and in the matter of returning lost property.

B. But a woman takes precedence over a man in the matter of [providing] clothing and redemption from captivity.

C. When both of them are standing in danger of defilement, the man takes precedence over the woman.

3:8

A. A priest takes precedence over a Levite, a Levite over an Israelite, an Israelite over a *mamzer* [the child of parents forbidden by the law of the Torah to marry, e.g., a brother and a sister, or a married woman and someone other than her husband], a *mamzer* over a *Netin* [the descendant of a family of Temple servants], a *Netin* over a proselyte, a proselyte over a freed slave.

B. Under what circumstances?

C. When all of them are equivalent.

D. But if the *mamzer* was a disciple of a sage and a high priest was an *am haares* [a person unlettered in the Torah learned through discipleship to a sage], the *mamzer* who is a disciple of a sage takes precedence over a high priest who is an *am haares*.
— Mishnah-tractate Horayot 3:6–8

I can imagine no clearer way of setting forth the entire message of the system of classical Judaism than this passage, which treats even the holiest officials of the Temple itself as subordinate, in the social order, to Torah-learning. That is why, as a matter of course, family relationships also are subordinated to those relationships with God that Torah-study realizes. But, as we shall now see, when the husband discovers the Torah and determines to devote his life to Torah-study, what happens to the wife and family is not to be ignored. They, too, bear the burden of the discovery, but also share in the reward. Once more, the social foundations of the religious life of the individual form part of the story of the turning, or conversion. That is because what is at stake in the Torah is God's presence in Israel, understood as the supernatural community called into being by God at Sinai, the holy people — and the people is made up of families, not of isolated individuals.

Certainly, the greatest sage in the generations that laid the foundations for the documents that contain the Oral Torah is Aqiba, and of him, as of Eliezer, is told the story of beginnings as a mature man who discovers his own ignorance. And the contribution of his wife and family forms an integral part of the account. We have several components of the tale, the first involving Aqiba on his own:

VI:V.1

A. How did R. Aqiba begin [his Torah-study]?

B. They say: He was forty years old and had never repeated a tradition [of the Oral Torah]. One time he was standing at the mouth of a well. He thought to himself, "Who carved out this stone?"

C. They told him, "It is the water that is perpetually falling on it every day."

D. They said to him, "Aqiba, do you not read Scripture? 'The water wears away stones' (Job 4:19)?"

E. On the spot R. Aqiba constructed in his own regard an argument *a fortiori:* now if something soft can wear down something hard, words of Torah, which are as hard as iron, how much the more so should it wear down my heart, which is made of flesh and blood.

Here we see a figure comparable to Saul/Paul, that is, one concerned with the sinful condition of the heart ("the good that I would...."). What will wear down the heart, purify it, make the heart — that is, a person's will — conform to the model, the image that God has consulted in making humanity? It is Torah-learning. That is what will purify the heart, and a later sage in the Talmud would make the matter explicit: "The All-Merciful craves the heart." That is why the language of "turning" or "repentance" takes over when Aqiba's decision to study the Torah is announced:

F. On the spot he repented [and undertook] to study the Torah.

Here we see in so many words that Torah-study marks a turning, an act of repentance. And what is at stake is made explicit when, in Tractate Abot, the sayings of the founders, it is said, "An ignorant person cannot be pious." But learning demands humility, and Aqiba shows what humility means when he becomes his son's fellow student, sharing the same kindergarten teacher:

G. He and his son went into study-session before a children's teacher, saying to him, "My lord, teach me Torah."

H. R. Aqiba took hold of one end of the tablet, and his son took hold of the other end. The teacher wrote out for him Alef Bet and he learned it, Alef Tav and he learned it, the Torah of the Priests [the books of Leviticus and Numbers] and he learned it. He went on learning until he had learned the entire Torah.

Then the same turning to the Torah requires capacity not only to master the words of the Torah but, especially, the power to reason intelligently: to enter into the processes of thought that yield the facts and results recorded in the documents that put down in permanent formulations the teachings of the Oral Torah:

> I. He went and entered study-sessions before R. Eliezer and before R. Joshua. He said to them, "My lords, open up for me the reasoning of the Mishnah."

> J. When they had stated one passage of law, he went and sat by himself and said, "Why is this alef written? Why is this bet written? Why is this statement made?" He went and asked them and, in point of fact, reduced them to silence.

VI:V.2

> A. R. Simeon b. Eleazar says, "I shall make a parable for you. To what is the matter comparable? To a stonecutter who was cutting stone in a quarry. One time he took his chisel and went and sat down on the mountain and started to chip away little sherds from it. People came by and said to him, 'What are you doing?'"

> B. "He said to them, 'Lo, I am going to uproot the mountain and move it into the Jordan River.'"

> C. "They said to him, 'You will never be able to uproot the entire mountain.'"

> D. "He continued chipping away at the mountain until he came to a huge boulder. He quarried underneath it and unearthed it and uprooted it and tossed it into the Jordan.

> E. "He said to the boulder, 'This is not your place, but that is your place.'

> F. "Likewise this is what R. Aqiba did to R. Eliezer and to R. Joshua."

Through his simple questions of a fundamental order, Aqiba investigated the foundations of the teachings of the greatest masters of his time, Eliezer, whom we met just now, and Joshua, his colleague. And Aqiba won the approbation of another of his teachers, Tarfon:

VI:V.3

A. Said R. Tarfon to him, "Aqiba, in your regard Scripture says, 'He stops up streams so that they do not trickle, and what is hidden he brings into the light' (Job 28:11)."

B. "Things that are kept as mysteries from ordinary people has R. Aqiba brought to light."

No one promises a life of ease for the disciple of sages. On the contrary, Aqiba made do with the cheapest fuel, the poorest food. And this leads us directly to the question, what happens to the wife and children of the one who turns to the Torah and begins study?

VI:V.4

A. Every day he would bring a bundle of twigs, half of which he would sell in exchange for food, and half of which he would use for a garment.

B. His neighbors said to him, "Aqiba, you are killing us with the smoke. Sell them to us, buy oil with the money, and by the light of a lamp do your studying."

C. He said to them, "I fill many needs with that bundle, first, I repeat traditions [by the light of the fire I kindle with] them, second, I warm myself with them, third, I sleep on them."

VI:V.5

A. In time to come R. Aqiba is going to impose guilt [for failing to study] on the poor [who use their poverty as an excuse not to study].

B. For if they say to them, "Why did you not study the Torah?" and they reply, "Because we were poor," they will say to them, "But was not R. Aqiba poorer and more poverty-stricken?"

C. If they say, "Because of our children [whom we had to work to support]," they will say to them, "Did not R. Aqiba have sons and daughters?"

D. So they will say to them, "Because Rachel, his wife, had the merit [of making it possible for him to study, and we have no equivalent helpmates; our wives do not have equivalent merit at their disposal]."

The reward of the wife comes about — in a world long ago and far away from the revolution in women's place in the social order that has taken place in the nineteenth and twentieth centuries — through her patience and endurance during her husband's absence. This marks the end of the story begun with Aqiba's turning to the Torah, and, as we see in a moment, forms the heart of a tale on its own:

VI:V.6

A.   It was at the age of forty that he went to study the Torah. Thirteen years later he taught the Torah in public.

B.   They say that he did not leave this world before there were silver and golden tables in his possession,

C.   and before he went up onto his bed on golden ladders.

D.   His wife went about in golden sandals and wore a golden tiara of the silhouette of the city [Jerusalem].

E.   His disciples said to him, "My lord, you have shamed us by what you have done for her [since we cannot do the same for our wives]."

F.   He said to them, "She bore a great deal of pain on my account for [the study of] the Torah."

— The Fathers according to Rabbi Nathan vi:v

A separate account of Aqiba's beginnings places Aqiba's wife at the center of his turning to Torah-study. He was a simple shepherd, of good character, and his boss's wife offered to accept betrothal with him on the condition that he go off and study the Torah. The father disinherited her for her action. Aqiba's wife — she is given no name — embodies the virtue of the wife who accepts the status of widow, so that her husband may stay away from home for long periods of Torah-study. What we deal with is a kind of jointly lived monastic life, the end of sexual relations for unconscionable periods of time, for the sake of Torah-study:

A.   R. Aqiba was the shepherd of Ben Kalba Sabua. His daughter saw that he was chaste and noble. She said to him, "If we become betrothed to you, will you go to the schoolhouse?"

B.   He said to her, "Yes."

C.   She became betrothed to him secretly and sent him off.

D.   Her father heard and drove her out of his house and forbade her by vow from enjoying his property.

E. He went and remained at the session for twelve years at the school-house. When he came back, he brought with him twelve thousand disciples. He heard a sage say to her, "How long [63A] are you going to lead the life of a life-long widow?"

F. She said to him, "If he should pay attention to me, he will spend another twelve years in study."

G. He said, "So what I'm doing is with permission." He went back and stayed in session another twelve years at the schoolhouse.

H. When he came back, he brought with him twenty-four thousand disciples. His wife heard and went out to meet him. Her neighbors said to her, "Borrow some nice clothes and put them on."

I. She said to them, "'A righteous man will recognize the soul of his cattle' (Prov. 12:10)."

J. When she came to him, she fell on her face and kissed his feet. His attendants were going to push her away. He said to them, "Leave her alone! What is mine and what is yours is hers."

K. Her father heard that an eminent authority had come to town. He said, "I shall go to him. Maybe he'll release me from my vow." He came to him [Aqiba]. He said to him, "Did you take your vow with an eminent authority in mind [as your son-in-law]?"

L. He said to him, "Even if he had known a single chapter, even if he had known a single law [I would never have taken that vow]!"

M. He said to him, "I am the man."

N. He fell on his face and kissed his feet and gave him half of his property.

O. The daughter of R. Aqiba did the same with Ben Azzai, and that is in line with what people say: "A ewe copies a ewe, a daughter's acts are like the mother's."

— Bavli-tractate Ketubot 5:6 vi.8./62b

The paradigm of "turning to Torah-study" now is fully exposed: poverty, rejection by one's family, long periods of hard work, but an ultimate reward: "I am the man." But the center of the story is the wife's superhuman, supernatural sacrifice — everything so that her man can study the Torah — and the just reward that came to her in the end.

Yet another story of Aqiba's discovery of the Torah underscores the poverty and virtue of the disciple and his wife. Now Aqiba and his wife live together the life of penury that Torah-study requires. However little they have, they find someone who has less; they learn the meaning of what they have; the wife then sends the husband away to study.

A. R. Aqiba became betrothed to the daughter of Kalba Sabua. Her father heard and drove her out of his house and forbade her by vow from enjoying his property.

B. They went and married him in winter. He would have to pick the straw out of his hair. He said to her, "If I had the money, I would give you a tiara of Jerusalem made out of gold."

C. Elijah came. He appeared to them in the form of a man, crying at the door, "Give me some straw, for my wife is in labor, and I don't have anything for her to lie on."

D. R. Aqiba said to his wife, "See, here is a man who doesn't even have straw."

E. She said to him, "Go into the household of a master."

Now the familiar story picks up, with some embellishments:

F. He went and spent twelve years before R. Eliezer and R. Joshua. At the end of this time, he came home. From the back of the house, he heard a wicked man ridiculing his wife, "Your father did right by you, first, that he is not equivalent to you in standing, second, he has left you a living widow all these years."

G. She said to him, "If he should pay attention to me, he will spend another twelve years in study."

H. He said, "So what I'm doing is with permission." He went back and stayed in session another twelve years at the schoolhouse.

I. When he came back, he brought with him twenty-four thousand pairs of disciples. Everybody went out to greet him, and she, too, went out to meet him.

J. The same wicked man said to her, "Where are you going?" Her neighbors said to her, "Borrow some nice clothes and put them on."

L. She said to him, " 'A righteous man will recognize the soul of his cattle' (Prov. 12:10)."

M. Then she came to him, but his attendants were going to push her away. He said to them, "Leave her alone! What is mine and what is yours is hers."

N. When her father heard of it, he came before him to seek release from his vow. He released his vow.

— BAVLI-TRACTATE NEDARIM 6:1 III.13/50B

Discovering the Torah requires different quests of different people. What makes Aqiba's discovery remarkable is that his wife motivated him to go in quest. Torah-study in community hardly refers to an abstraction — the formation of a supernatural family in place of the natural, this-worldly one. Torah-study encompasses the family, the son along with the father, and it comes about by reason of the devotion of the wife and daughters as well. In contemporary Judaism, with women studying the Torah in yeshivas and seminaries, the wheel has come full circle, and the question posed by the wife of Aqiba has found its logical answer: Why not you?

So in this account of the spirituality of Judaism in the encounter with God, we end where we began, with the recognition that spirituality finds its form and meaning in Torah-learning. The Torah is given ("revealed") by God in the act of self-manifestation. So the Torah itself proclaims its own origins in Heaven: "I am the Lord your God...," "The Lord spoke to Moses, saying, 'Speak to the children of Israel and say to them...,'" "I will make all my goodness pass before you and will proclaim before you my name, 'The Lord,' and I will be gracious to whom I will be gracious and will show mercy on whom I will show mercy. But you cannot see my face." These and companion proclamations leave no doubt for holy Israel that in the Torah is God: the record of God's call to humanity through holy Israel. Israel receives the Torah to meet God and in the Torah Israel's encounter with God takes place.

So to encounter the spirituality of holy Israel, come to a synagogue on a Sabbath, Monday, or Thursday, or on a holy day or festival, and you will hear the Torah not read but sung, loud and clear, in ancient chant, melody matching natural sounds of the very words God says. The song of the Torah ordinarily is sung with great punctiliousness. It is solely to hear the Torah declaimed that holy Israel is summoned to the synagogue. Most of the rest of the liturgy may be recited at home, in private, in thick silence. The Torah defines the sole, obligatory public event. This is so not only for what the Torah says in God's behalf, but what Israel says in response. Specifically, once the Torah is removed from its holy ark, carried in choreographed parade around the synagogue, the scroll is held up. At that sight of the unfurled columns of the scroll displayed before it, in response the congregation sings back, "This is the Torah that Moses set before the children of Israel at the command of the Lord." Then, and only then, holy Israel having announced itself as present, the Torah is sung out to the people. So it goes week by week, through the year: "In the beginning God created the heaven and the earth..." through "And there arose not a prophet since in Israel like unto Moses, whom the Lord knew face to face...." So goes the song of the Torah from Genesis through Deuteronomy, song out of the scroll of the Torah. To that, everything else forms massive commentary.

Or encounter the spirituality of holy Israel and go to an academy and stand against the wall and listen to the cacophony, as disciples young and old shout at each other in animated (also ritualized) argument, and you will soon hear the inner rhythm of the shouts and grasp that they are not yelling at one another but singing to one another. In fact there is a pattern, a sing-song; not an array of civil arguments, calmly put forth for reasoned argument and decision, but an explosion of violent sound, crescendos of phrases, rivers of words, all of them flowing in a powerful current, deeply felt, sincerely meant: the stakes are high. So the men shout at one another, singing to one another, the chant bearing the signals of the sort of argument that is being mounted, the conventions of thought that are being replayed.

But shouting and shrieking mark the location and shape sound all the rest of the time. This one proposes, that one disposes. This one forms a proposition in response to what the Torah (here: the Mishnah, the Talmud, or a later commentator) says, and that one says why what this one says is wrong: here are the flaws. If you are right, then I shall show the absurd consequence that follows. If you maintain thus-and-so, I shall demonstrate the disharmonies that result. Your music is my cacophony, your melody, my disharmony. And then you sing back, "No, because," or "Yes, but," and I sing back: an endless exchange of voices. All the time, we are held together in our argument by shared conviction that what is at stake is truth, not power, nor personalities, nor even the merely formal rituals of an empty academicism such as we may see acted out on an academic stage here or there. But the sages knew that and condemned it when they told Mr. Five-Sins that from him they learned Torah. For study of the Torah constitutes an act of spirituality: a quest for God where God is to be found.

Meeting Christ: God with Us, with Christ

Come on, toward me all who labor and are burdened, and I will provide you repose. Take my yoke on yourselves, and learn from me, because I am gentle and humble in heart, and you will find repose for your lives. Because my yoke is useful and my burden is slight.

— THE GOSPEL ACCORDING TO ST. MATTHEW 11:28–29

The Perspective of the Gospel according to Matthew, and Jesus' Practice

Jesus' invitation in Matthew's Gospel is a direct offer to change the conditions of life for those who hear him. Laboring, being burdened: these are the facts of our existence. For those to whom these words are directed, in Galilee, these are facts, not metaphors. Galileans worked land that was tenanted to them. But because their economy was based principally on the exchange of goods and services among them, not on financial transactions of currency, they were persistently in debt.[1] Labor and burden could seem without end as a definition of one's life.

Matthew's Gospel, composed around the year 80 C.E., probably in Damascus, was produced in different circumstances, in the bustling conditions of a cosmopolitan city under Roman hegemony.[2] Those who first heard this Gospel understood themselves to be part of a "church," an *ekklesia* in Greek. That term initially meant a congregation or assembly, corresponding to a *kenneset* in Hebrew, which comes to be rendered

---

1. See Richard Horsley, *Archaeology, History, and Society in Galilee* (Valley Forge, Pa.: Trinity Press International, 1996).

2. See John McRay, "Damascus. The Greco-Roman Period," *The Anchor Bible Dictionary* (ed. D. N. Freedman and others; New York: Doubleday, 1992) 2.7–8.

in English as a synagogue (from *sunagôgê* in Greek). It is in Matthew, alone of all the Gospels, that "church" appears in sayings of Jesus, most strikingly in a foundational promise (Matt. 16:17–19):

> You are favored, Shimon bar Yonah, because flesh and blood did not uncover this for you, but my father who is in the heavens! And I say to you that you are Rock, and upon this rock I will build my congregation, and Hades' gates will not prevail over it. I will give you the keys of the sovereignty of the heavens, and whatever you bind upon the earth shall have been bound in the heavens, and whatever you loose upon the earth shall have been loosed in the heavens.

The power of the Church resides in its capacity to "loose" those very burdens that Jesus had spoken of, and especially to release its members from the consequences of their sin.

When we put together Jesus' promise of repose and his authorization of forgiveness to his Church, a double transition becomes evident in the presentation of Matthew. The more obvious transition has already emerged: the conditions of the rural, subsistence economy of Galilee are transposed to those of metropolitan Damascus. But what is obvious may also be profound: Christian spirituality refuses any attempt to begin from any position except our recognition that we are those "who labor and are burdened." Humanity itself involves an awareness of constraint, each of us with our own sort of indebtedness to account for, and finding ourselves caught short in that accounting. Attempts to pretend to begin from a position of strength are rebuffed, right across the spectrum of Christian opinion. Paul wrote with biting sarcasm to Christians in Corinth around 56 C.E. (1 Cor. 4:8):

> Already you are sated! Already you have become rich! Apart from us — you reign! And you indeed should reign, so that we might reign with you!

In its ethos and theology, the letter of James contrasts with Paul's overall position, but it is no less trenchant in its more straightforward condemnation of any pretense of strength on the basis of social status (James 5:1–3):

> Accordingly now, wail you rich, crying aloud over your coming distresses. Your wealth has rotted, and your garments have become moth-eaten; your gold and your silver have corroded, and their

poison will be for witness against you and will eat your flesh, as a fire you have stored up in final days.

The criticism of wealth is not only a social teaching from the earliest days of Christianity. The focus of the critique is the pride that people might take in possessions or in positions of honor. It is the claim of some Corinthians to an exalted station on the basis of social position (1 Cor. 1:18) which occasions Paul's scorn, the pretensions of the wealthy to positions of honor in the congregation (James 2:1–13) which brings on the diatribe in the name of James.

The acknowledgement of one's mortal position and the fact of the constraints in which one lives are taken as the prelude to a transforming encounter with God. Both Matthew and Luke (composed around the year 90 C.E., in Antioch) attest that conviction within sayings attributed to Jesus in varying idioms (Matt. 5:1–12; Luke 6:20–26):

He saw the crowds and went up into the mountain, and when he had sat down his students came forward. He opened his mouth and was teaching them, saying, "The poor in spirit are favored, because theirs is the sovereignty of the heavens; Mourners are favored, because *they* will be comforted; The gentle are favored, because *they* will inherit the earth; Those who hunger and thirst for righteousness are favored, because *they* will be satisfied; The merciful are favored, because *they* will receive mercy; The pure in heart are favored, because *they* will see God; The peacemakers are favored, because *they* will be called descendants of God; Those persecuted on account of righteousness are favored, because theirs is the sovereignty of the heavens. You are favored, when they reproach you and persecute you and, lying, say every evil against you on my account. Rejoice and celebrate! Because your reward is great in the heavens; for so they persecuted the prophets before you."

He personally lifted up his eyes towards his students and was saying, "The poor are favored, because *yours* is the sovereignty of God; Those who hunger now are favored, because you will be satisfied; Those who weep now are favored, because you will laugh; You are favored, when humanity hates you and when they exclude you and reproach you and throw out your name as evil on the one like the person's account. Rejoice in that day and skip, for look: your reward is great in the heaven; for their fathers did the same things to the prophets. Except: Miseries to you rich, because you possess your consolation; Miseries to you, who are filled up now, because you will hunger; Miseries, who laugh now, because who will mourn and weep; Miseries, when all humanity speaks well of you, for their fathers did the same things to the false prophets."

For all that there are significant differences between these two presen-tations, they both turn on a single axis: the paradox Jesus insists on, that God's sovereignty is bestowed just where power, in human terms, is least.

To an important extent, this dominical paradox (which Jesus generated, but was also attributed to the risen Christ) is grounded in well-established expectations of justice for the poor in the book of Psalms. Psalm 35:10 is representative, but also riveting in its resonance with dominical teaching: "All my bones shall say, 'LORD, who is like you, delivering the poor from one stronger than he, the poor and needy from his robber?'" This psalm as a whole is a plea for vindication and an anticipation that such a moment of justice is to come, so as to be celebrated in Israel's worship. The language of poverty, in other words, is applied, as in the dominical teaching of Christianity, to the situation of being human as such.

Both the psalms and the dominical tradition anticipate that a moment of divine disclosure will remedy the poverty of our spirits. For the psalmist, that moment is when the LORD judges (so Ps. 35:24): "Judge me, LORD my God, according to my righteousness, And let them not rejoice over me." Vindication for the just, here, is also to include judgment of the oppressors (Ps. 35:4): "Let them be put to shame and brought to dishonor that seek after my life." The theme of judgment is also one of the vital dimensions of Jesus' reference to the sovereignty (or kingdom) of God.[3] The portrayal of God as sovereign within the Psalms obviously was an influence upon Jesus. But in addition, the language of divine sovereignty was applied within the Aramaic Targums to refer to the moment of vindication which the Psalms anticipated and longed for. An example of that usage is provided at Isa. 24:23 in the Isaiah Targum, and the resonance with our theme of judgment as sounded in the Psalm just cited is notable:[4]

> Then *those who serve* the moon will be *ashamed* and *those who worship* the sun will be *humiliated; for the sovereignty of* the LORD *of* hosts *will be revealed* on *the* Mount *of* Zion and in Jerusalem and before the elders *of* his *people in* glory.

---

3. See Chilton, *Pure Kingdom. Jesus' Vision of God: Studying the Historical Jesus 1* (Eerdmans: Grand Rapids and London: SPCK, 1996) 36–38 (on the book of Psalms), 74–80 (on Jesus' teaching).

4. The translation is taken from Chilton, *The Isaiah Targum. Introduction, Translation, Apparatus, and Notes: The Aramaic Bible 11* (Wilmington: Glazier and Edinburgh: Clark, 1987). For a full discussion of the correspondence between dominical teaching and the Isaiah Targum, see Idem, *A Galilean Rabbi and His Bible. Jesus' Use of the Interpreted Scripture of His Time* (Wilmington: Glazier, 1984) 216 pp.; also published with the subtitle, *Jesus' own interpretation of Isaiah* (London: SPCK, 1984).

By the time of Jesus, it is apparent that the psalmic language of vindication had been taken up within the expectation and celebration of divine sovereignty.

But among all the rabbis of his time, and times earlier and later, none is attested to have focused on the divine sovereignty as much as Jesus did. That focus went hand in hand with his characteristic practice. This practice was carefully crafted and developed into a form which Jesus' disciples could apprehend. Their apprehension was of a Kabbalah, a tradition of ascent to God, where divine vindication could be known and experienced.

The Kabbalah of Rabbi Jesus

Why speak of Kabbalah, and then link that to Jesus? The "Kabbalah," as that term is commonly used, refers to a movement of Jewish mysticism from the twelfth century through the Renaissance (in its initial flowering).[5] Its focus was on the mystical union with God, in a way analogous to the paths advocated by Christian mystics such as Julian of Norwich and Johannes Eckhart. Its character included an intellectual discipline, literary focus on the precise wording of the Torah, and even an academic rigor in the description of the divine spheres into which the initiate was to enter with great care. What relation might that have to a rabbi of the first century from Galilee, whose attainments did not include the ability even to write, and whose own references to the Hebrew Bible were so imprecise as to indicate he was illiterate?

Although Kabbalah indeed can be used with a restrictive meaning, its underlying orientation is nothing other than the approach of God's Merkabah, the heavenly chariot throne from which divine power and wisdom emanated for the ordering of all creation. The conception of that Merkabah is much more ancient, profoundly rooted in the theology of Israel, than the development of kabbalistic techniques during the Middle Ages. Indeed, the ascent to the divine throne is older than Israel itself.

From Mesopotamia, from the twenty-third century B.C.E. and the fifteenth century C.E., stories are told of kings and courtiers entering into

---

5. See Gershom Scholem, "Kabbalah," *Encyclopedia Judaica* 10 (Jerusalem: Keter, 1972) 489–653 and the fine introduction of Joseph Dan in *The Early Kabbalah: The Classics of Western Spirituality* (New York: Paulist, 1986) 1–41. Among many more recent works, reference should be made to Moshe Idel, *Kabbalah. New Perspectives* (New Haven and London: Yale University Press, 1988) and Elliott R. Wolfson, *Through a Speculum that Shines. Vision and Imagination in Medieval Jewish Mysticism* (Princeton: Princeton University Press, 1994).

the palace of heaven and receiving visions and empowerment there.[6] Israel learned these royal traditions from Babylonia and converted them into prophetic authorization, especially during the time of Ezekiel (in the sixth century B.C.E.). Ezekiel himself related his classic vision of the throne of God as a chariot, a Merkabah, and what is usually called Merkabah mysticism derives from his vision (in Ezekiel 1). After Ezekiel, the book of Daniel (chapter 7) detailed this vision further (during the second century B.C.E.). And in the time of Jesus, the book of Enoch, found in fragments in Aramaic at Qumran, took that tradition further.

The book of Genesis says of Enoch only that "he walked with God, and he was not" (Gen. 5:22). This disappearance is taken as a sign that Enoch enjoyed a vision by ascent into the multiple heavens above the earth and was authorized to relate its wisdom to Israel, indeed to act as an intermediary to the angels who had disobeyed God. From Ezekiel, through Daniel and Enoch and on to John the Baptist and Jesus, there is a growing tradition, a kabbalah (something received),[7] which reflects a deep commitment to the disciplined practice of the vision of God's throne. The fragments of Enoch at Qumran are found in Aramaic, which suggests that the book was used, not just by the Essenes (who tended to guard their sectarian documents in Hebrew), but by a wider audience, which included the Essenes.[8] In fact, the book of Enoch is also quoted at a later stage in the New Testament, so that there can be no doubt of its widespread use. Another work found in Hebrew at Qumran and widely attested elsewhere, the book of Jubilees, also presents Enoch as a figure of revelation: he himself knows the Torah later communicated to Moses by angelic communication.

The development of these traditions is obviously not independent: there is a successive building and borrowing from one to the other. The ascent to the divine throne was an aspiration which was "received" or "taken," one source from others. To "receive" or to "take" in both Aramaic and Hebrew is expressed by the verb *qabal*, from which the noun *qabbalah* is derived, and the noun is used in both Mishnah and Talmud to refer to ancient tradition, including the Prophets and the Writings

---

6. See Bernhard Lang, "Die grosse Jenseitsfahrt," *Paragana* 7.2 (1998) 24–42, 32. See Stephanie Dally, *Myths from Mesopotamia* (Oxford: 1989) 182–187 and James D. Tabor, "Heaven, Ascent to," *Anchor Bible Dictionary* (ed. D. N. Freedman and others: New York: Doubleday, 1992) 3.91–94.

7. At a much later stage, this mystical tradition was formalized into the academic complexity of the Medieval Kabbalah, which was a learned and intellectual movement.

8. For an introduction and translation, see E. Isaac, "1 Enoch," *The Old Testament Pseudepigrapha* (ed. J. H. Charlesworth; Garden City: Doubleday, 1983) I.5–89.

within the Bible of Israel (as distinct from the Torah).[9] Now what is *qabaled* might be any sort of authoritative tradition, but it is tradition concerning the Merkabah which is our concern here. When Paul wishes to underline the authority of his teaching concerning the eucharist, he says, "For I received from the Lord what I also delivered over to you," and he goes on to speak of both Jesus' last meal with his followers and its significance and correct observance (1 Cor. 11:23–33). The sources of Paul's authority include what he learned from primitive Christians (especially Peter, see Gal. 1:18), but more importantly what he calls the *apokalypsis*, the uncovering, of Christ Jesus (Gal. 1:12):

> For I want to inform you, fellows, of the message messaged by me, that it is not by a person. For I neither received it from a person, nor was I taught, but through an uncovering of Messiah Jesus.

That disclosure occurred in a supernatural realm, the third heaven, the paradise to which Paul says he was snatched up, where he was told unutterable wisdoms (2 Cor. 12:1–4).[10]

Such language is not merely formal or rhetorical; it is also a matter of spiritual practice. Paul is attesting, at the generative moment of his identity as an apostle, that the vision of the divine throne to which the risen Jesus had been elevated was at the heart of his own experience. There is no trace of Paul's famous tendency toward argumentation here: the practice of ascent is simply taken to be understood among those who first heard his letters. The assurance of Paul that this ascent was a self-evident aspect of his authorization invites us to look back, to seek traces of the power of the Merkabah in the experience of Jesus. Those traces are perhaps most plain in Jesus' baptism, and in what that reception of the Holy Spirit produced in him. That takes us back to Jesus' association with John called the "immerser" (the *baptistes* in Greek, from the verb *baptizomai*, which means "immerse").

Many people came to John for this immersion, most often on the way to the Temple along the well-established path of pilgrimage that followed the Jordan Valley. Once they arrived at the base of the mount of the Temple in Jerusalem itself, they would be confronted by a bewildering array of differing kinds of purification — of varying degrees of expense — and every pilgrim would have to negotiate passage up to the double

---

9. See the article appended to Scholem's, *Encyclopedia Judaica* 10 (Jerusalem: Keter, 1972) 653–654.

10. See Victor Paul Furnish, *II Corinthians: The Anchor Bible* (Garden City: Doubleday, 1984) 542–545.

gate. But even before arrival there, enthusiastic pilgrims wanted to know themselves as part of Israel, the people of God. Immersions such as John's provided them with a sense of confidence and integrity. From the writings of Josephus, we know that John was not the only such figure; Josephus refers to his own study with another immerser, named Bannus.[11] The pilgrims' local *miqveh* (immersion pool, if they even had access to one) might not correspond to the Pharisaic design and would be much less luxurious than those of the Sadducees, less elaborate than those of the Essenes. But John offered them purification in God's own water and the assurance that this was the practice of Israel's true purity. Then what they faced in Jerusalem was less daunting; the claims and counterclaims of various factions would be put into perspective by the confidence that one had already been purified by God's own living waters.

Immersion, for John, was no once-for-all act, as in later Christian baptism. In the practice of the primitive Church, after the resurrection, believers felt that they received the Spirit of God when they were immersed in the name of Jesus. That conviction was only possible after the resurrection, because it stemmed from the belief that Jesus was alive and at the right hand of God, so as to be able to dispense divine Spirit. In Peter's speech at Pentecost (the Magna Charta of baptismal theology), Jesus, having been exalted to the right hand of God, receives the promise of the Holy Spirit from the Father and pours it out on his followers (Acts 2:33). Once received by a Christian, that spirit did not come and go. Subsequent immersion could not top up a lack of Spirit. A Christian lived in the power of God's Spirit; its influence might increase or decrease, but the fact of its presence was irrevocable. But in John's practice, as in Judaism as a whole, purification was a routine requirement, and people might return to John many times, and they naturally engaged in many forms of purification other than John's, whether in their villages or at the Temple. Impurity was a fact of life and, therefore, so was purification. But John was there in the wilderness to attest that the natural, living water provided by God would achieve acceptability before God, provided that immersion was accompanied by repentance.[12]

But for the *talmidim* (that is, the disciples) of John, this continual immersion — as well as the immersion of others — was more than a

---

11. See Josephus' *Life* §11. For my discussion of John, Bannus, and their methods of purification as related to Jesus, see *Jesus' Baptism and Jesus' Healing: His Personal Practice of Spirituality* (Trinity Press International, 1998).

12. See Joan Taylor, *The Immerser: John the Baptist within Second Temple Judaism: Studying the Historical Jesus* (Grand Rapids: Eerdmans, 1997).

matter of simple repentance. Within that activity, there was an esoteric meaning. John conveyed a definite understanding of the final significance which his purification for Israel offered. The sources are plain: for John, immersion brought one to the point that one could understand what God was about to do with Israel. As John himself expressed it, immersing oneself in water prepared one to receive the Spirit of God himself, which was to drench all Israel with its sanctification. The key to John's preparation for God himself lies in the wording attributed to him, "I immerse you in water, but he himself will immerse you in Holy Spirit" (Mark 1:8; see Matt. 3:11; Luke 3:16). Within the context of Christianity after the resurrection, those words are fulfilled by what the risen Jesus endows the believer with; but that assumes Jesus' identification with God at that point, because only God himself can give of his own Spirit. Within the context of John the immerser, however, what is at issue is the purification which prepares the way for divine Spirit. The link between purification with water and the vindicating presence of God's Spirit is explicitly made in the book of Ezekiel, the same book which is the *locus classicus* of the Merkabah (Ezek. 36:22–27):

> Therefore, say to the house of Israel: So says the Lord, the LORD: Not for your sake am I acting, house of Israel, but for my holy name, which you have profaned among the peoples you came to. I will sanctify my great name, although profaned among the peoples among whom you have profaned it, and the peoples will know that I am the LORD, says the Lord, the LORD, when I am sanctified among you before their eyes. I will take you from the peoples, and gather you from all the lands, and bring you to your land. I will sprinkle on you clean waters and cleanse you from all your uncleannesses and from all your idols I will cleanse you. I will give you a new heart and a new spirit I will put in you midst, and remove the heart of stone from your flesh and give you a heart of flesh. My Spirit I shall put in your midst and I will make you walk according to my statutes and keep my judgments and do them.

The close and causal connection between water and Spirit here has led to the insight that we have here an important Scriptural precedent of John's immersion.[13] Everything that divided Israel, that prevented it from realizing the full promise of the covenant, was to be swept away by

---

13. See Otto Böcher, "Johannes der Täufer," *Theologische Realenzyklopädie* 17 (1988) 172–181, 175. This insight, suggested to me by Bernhard Lange, is worked out more fully in *Jesus' Baptism and Jesus' Healing.*

the power of the Spirit. Those who were urged to repent, the pilgrims of Israel and their companions, were told of the impending judgment which the coming of God's Spirit necessarily involved. After all, God's Spirit proceeded from his throne, the source of all true judgment.

John practiced a *kabbalah* of envisioning the throne of God, which backed up his practice of immersion. He and his *talmidim* saw the Spirit of God before his throne, ready to drench Israel, just as Israel was drenched in the waters of purification. The careful discipline of these *talmidim*, their repetitive, committed practice, their sometimes inadequate diet and exposure to the elements, all contributed to the vividness of their visions of God's throne. It was suggested some years ago by John Allegro that the ingestion of psychotropic mushrooms was a part of this discipline.[14] While the influence of herbs and grasses, as well as mushrooms, on people's psychological state cannot be discounted, the greater influence of these visions was the *kabbalah* itself, its intentional recollection and envisioning of the throne of God. From Qumran a fragment praises God as the apex of a heavenly panoply:

> He is God of gods of all the heads of the heights and king of kings
> for all eternal councils.[15]

The foundation of kabbalah is putting the intent of the mind into envisaging the heavenly throne.

Jesus' skill in this vision made him one of John's most prominent *talmidim*, but it also led to Jesus' break with John. The Gospels all relate the baptism of Jesus in a way which adumbrates baptism in early Christianity. But they also refer to the particular vision of Jesus, which not every baptized Christian could or did claim (Matt. 3:13–17; Mark 1:9–13 Luke 3:21–22; see the facing page).

As Jesus was immersed for purification, he came to have an increasingly vivid vision, of the heavens splitting open, and God's Spirit coming upon him. And a voice: "You are my Son, beloved; in you I take pleasure." Each of these elements is resonant with the Israelite *kabbalah* of the divine throne.

---

14. *The Sacred Mushroom and the Cross. A Study of the Nature and Origins of Christianity within the Fertility Cults of the Ancient Near East* (Garden City: Doubleday, 1970). His suggestion that "Jesus" was simply a name for a mushroom assured Allegro a frosty reception, and his attempt to see Jesus as entirely mythical (indeed, hallucinatory) reads as a desperate attempt not to place him within historical context.

15. The fragment was found in the fourth cave from near Qumran (its designation is 4 Q403 frg. li). E. Glicker Chazon of Hebrew University in Jerusalem showed me a copy.

Matthew 3:13–17	*Mark 1:9–13*	*Luke 3:21–22*
[13]Then there came Yeshua from Galil to the Yordan to Yochanan to be immersed by him. [14]Yet he prevented him, saying, "I have need to be immersed by you, and do you come to me?" [15]Yeshua replied, and said to him, "Permit it now, for so it is proper for us to fulfill all righteousness." Then he permitted him. [16]Yet when Yeshua had been immersed, at once he came up from the water, and look: the heavens were opened, and he saw God's Spirit descending as a dove, coming upon him. [17]And look: a voice from the heavens, saying: "This is my beloved Son, in whom I take pleasure."	[9]And it happened in those days that there came Yeshua from Nazeret of Galil and he was immersed in the Yordan by Yochanan. [10]At once he came up from the water and saw the heavens splitting and the Spirit as a dove descending upon him. [11]And a voice came from the heavens: "You are my Son, beloved; in you I take pleasure." [12]And at once the Spirit threw him out into the wilderness. [13]And he was in the wilderness forty days, pressed to the limit by Satan; and he was with the animals, and the angels provided for him.	[21]But it happened when all the people were immersed, and Yeshua was immersed and praying, the heaven opened [22]and the Holy Spirit descended upon him in body, in form as a dove, and a voice came from heaven, "You are my Son, beloved; in you I take pleasure."

The heavens are viewed as multiple, hard shells above the earth, so that any real disclosure of the divine must represent a rending of those firmaments. But once opened, Jesus' vision is not of ascending through the heavens, as in the case of Enoch, but of the Spirit, as a dove, hovering over him and descending. That image is a vivid realization that the Spirit of God at creation once hovered over the face of the primeval waters (Gen. 1:2) as a bird. The bird was identified as a dove in Rabbinic tradition, and a fragment from Qumran supports the association.[16] The Spirit, which would one day come to Israel, in Jesus' vision was already upon him, and God took pleasure in him as a "son." The term "son" itself appears extremely frequently in the Old Testament, in order to speak of the special relationship between God and others. Angels can be called "sons of God," Israel is referred to as a divine son (most famously in Hos. 11:1), and the Davidic king can be assured by divine voice, "You are my son, this day have I begotten you!" (Ps. 2:7). All these are expressions,

---

16. See Dale C. Allison, "The Baptism of Jesus and a New Dead Sea Scroll," *Biblical Archaeology Review* 18.2 (1992) 58–60.

not of a biological relationship, but of the direct revelation which God extends to certain people and angels. Jesus claims that he is of their spiritual lineage within his embrace of John's *kabbalah.*

Jesus' vivid experience within his practice of John's immersion, a persistent vision occurring many times, may be contrasted with a story about Hillel, an older contemporary of Jesus'. He readily accepted a convert to Judaism and taught, "That which you hate, do not do to your fellow: that is the entire Torah, while all the rest is commentary thereon" (cf. Shabbath 31a).[17] Jesus took a similar point of view (Matt. 7:12; Luke 6:31) which is known as the Golden Rule. The same Hillel was held in such high esteem that he was thought worthy to receive the Holy Spirit. That estimate appears all the more exalted, but also strangely wistful, when it is borne in mind that the rabbis held that the Spirit had been withdrawn since the time of the last prophets of Scripture. These motifs are drawn together in a most exciting manner in a Rabbinic story:[18]

> Until the dead live, namely Haggai, Zechariah, and Malachi, the latter prophets, the Holy Spirit has ceased from Israel. Yet even so, they made them hear *bath qol.* An example: the sages gathered at the house of Guria in Jericho, and they heard a *bath qol* saying, There is here a man who is predestined for the Holy Spirit, except that his generation is not righteous for such. And they put their eyes on Hillel the elder, and when he died, they said of him, "Woe the meek man, Woe, the faithful disciple of Ezra."

With the withdrawal of Spirit until the prophets live again, God's favor is made known by an angelic echo, a *bath qol* ("daughter of a voice"). But the poignancy of this story is that, for all Hillel's merit, the Spirit itself is withheld. Jesus' approach to the Merkabah by means of John's *kabbalah* had opened the revolutionary prospect that the gates of heaven were open again for the Spirit to descend upon Israel.

Initially, Jesus' vision of the Merkabah is a special victory for John. He even referred to Jesus as "the lamb of God that takes away the sin of the world" (John 1:29, cf. v. 33). That phrase is attributed to John the immerser in the Gospel according to John in a passage which serves as a commentary on the meaning of Jesus' baptism. For the readers of John

---

17. The cleverness of Hillel's response to the request of the convert to be taught the Torah while he stood on one foot is manifest in the next sentence, "Go and learn it!" That is, he insists that the summary does not replace the commentary. In that regard, cf. Matt. 5:17.

18. Tosefta Sotah 13:3. (The Tosefta is a large supplement to the Mishnah, from the third century C.E.) For a discussion, see Chilton, *Profiles of a Rabbi. Synoptic Opportunities in Reading about Jesus: Brown Judaic Studies* 177 (Atlanta: Scholars Press, 1989) 77–89.

in the period after the Temple was destroyed in 70 C.E., that evoked a picture of Jesus as replacing sacrifice. But the earlier meaning was more humble and directly rooted in John's movement of baptismal forgiveness. He designated Jesus as a *talmid* who, young as a lamb, also wiped away so much sin that God's own Spirit could be felt as present within him. Jesus success as a baptist, an active immerser of other people, is also attested in John's Gospel (see John 3:22, 26). The Gospel subsequently attempts to correct that plain statement, by saying it was Jesus' *talmidim*, rather than Jesus himself, who baptized (John 4:1–3). But that is double anachronism: Jesus did not yet have his own *talmidim*, and he was not yet independent of John.

That Gospel, like the Synoptics, would prefer to forget that Jesus himself engaged in baptism. For them, the basic pattern was that John prepared the way by his baptism, and that Jesus followed as what was being prepared for. But, as a *talmid* of John's, Jesus' personal activity as an immerser was natural; that is why it is attested in the Gospel according to John (3:22, 26; 4:1). Jesus' success is such that it is brought to John the immerser's attention, who says in a stoic manner, "He must increase, and I must decrease" (John 3:30). But the tensions went much deeper than that remark can conceal. John's Gospel also speaks of a battle concerning "purification" (John 3:25) involving John and Jesus. That was at the heart of John's program and attests the break, which became all but inevitable.

Open antagonism develops between John and Jesus as Jesus moves out of John's stomping ground of the Jordan into settlement areas. He is baptizing more people than John, and he begins to assert that the people coming to cleanse themselves with John are in fact already clean. In Jesus' mind, repentance alone cleanses, so that Israelites who have repented can claim access to God, divine forgiveness, and divine support. The basis of Jesus' activity was his own experience while being himself immersed. He intensifies, extends, and generalizes John's teaching of the Merkabah.

The practice of fellowship in meals, celebrating sanctification, became more than a matter of happenstance in Jesus' activity at this time. Once he had celebrated makeshift feasts with hungry pilgrims. Now he actively sought out people in their hamlets and villages and towns around the Jordan and accepted hospitality from them in advance of immersing them. He was their guest, but he was also an itinerant rabbi, known by his association with John to offer purification. As he joined in the meal of *kiddush*, often celebrated, then and now on the eve of the Shabbat, Jesus or the elder host of the meal would speak of the sanctification of

God, who for Jesus was the Abba of all who turn to the source of Israel's blessing. In this reference to the Abba of Israel and his sanctification, major elements of the prayer Jesus later taught his own *talmidim* were taking shape and being brought together:

> Abba, your name will be sanctified,
> Your sovereignty will come.

At this stage, the prayer was not a form of words, but a thematic approach to God closely associated with the kiddush of God's sovereignty. What was being celebrated was not only the dawn of the Shabbat on its eve, but the dawn of the manifestation of God's glory.

Another case where stories concerning divine voices find resonance in the New Testament is the Transfiguration (Matt. 16:28–17:8; Mark 9:2–8; Luke 9:27–36), as seen on the facing page.

The narrative structure is reminiscent of Moses' ascent of Sinai in Exodus 24. At the close of that story, Moses is said to ascend the mountain, where God's glory, as a cloud, covered it (v. 15). The covering lasted six days (v. 16), which is the amount of time between the Transfiguration and the previous discourse in both Matthew (17:1) and Mark (9:2). After that time, the LORD calls to Moses from the cloud (Exod. 24:16b), and Moses entered the glory of the cloud, which is like a devouring fire (vv. 17–18). Earlier in the chapter, Moses is commanded to select three worshippers (Aaron, Nadab, and Abihu) together with seventy elders, in order to confirm the covenant (vv. 1–8). The result is that just these people (v. 9) see the God of Israel in his court (v. 10) and celebrate their vision with a meal. The motifs of master, three disciples, mountain, cloud, vision, and audition recur in the Transfiguration.

Other details in the presentation of the story cohere with Exodus 24. Matt. 17:2 uniquely refers to Jesus' face shining like the sun, like Moses' aspect in Exod. 34:29–35. In more general terms, Mark's reference to the whiteness of Jesus' garments also establishes a heavenly context. A variation in Luke is more specific and more interesting. Luke puts a distance of eight days, rather than six, between the previous discourse and the Transfiguration. Although that has baffled commentators, in Rabbinic interpretation that variation is meaningful. In the Targum Pseudo-Jonathan (Exod. 24:10–11), Nadab and Abihu are struck by God, because their vision contradicts the principle that "a human being will not see God and live" (Exod. 33:30). But their punishment (narrated in Num. 3:2–4) is delayed until the eighth day.

Matthew 16:28–17:8

28"Amen I say to you that there are some of those standing here, such as will never taste death until they see the one like the person coming in his sovereignty." 1And after six days Yeshua takes Rock and Ya'aqov and Yochanan his brother and brings them up to a high mountain privately. 2And he was transmuted before them and his face shone as the sun, and his clothing became white as the light. 3And look: there appeared to them Mosheh and Eliyah, speaking together with him. 4Rock responded and said to Yeshua, "Lord, it is good for us to be here; if you wish, I shall build here three lodges: one for you and one for Mosheh and one for Eliyah." 5While he was still speaking, look: a glowing cloud overshadowed them, and look: a voice from the cloud, saying, "This is my son, the beloved, in whom I take pleasure. Hear him." 6The students heard and fell on their faces and were exceedingly frightened. 7Yeshua came forward and touched them and said, "Be raised, and do not fear!" 8They lifted up their eyes and saw no one but him, Yeshua alone.

Mark 9:2–8

1And he was saying to them, "Amen I say to you that there are some here of those standing, such as will never taste death until they see the sovereignty of God having come in power." 2And after six days Yeshua takes Rock and Ya'aqov and Yochanan and brings them up to a high mountain privately: alone. 3And he was transmuted before them and his clothing became gleaming, very white, as a washer on the earth is not able to whiten. 4And Eliyah appeared to them with Mosheh, and they were speaking together with Yeshua. 5Rock responded and says to Yeshua, "Rabbi, it is good for us to be here, and we shall build three lodges: one for you and one for Mosheh and one for Eliyah." 6For he did not know how he should respond, because they were terrified. 7And a cloud came overshadowing them, and there came a voice from the cloud, "This is my son, the beloved: hear him." 8Suddenly looking around they no longer saw anyone with themselves but Yeshua, alone.

Luke 9:27–36

27"But I say to you truly, there are some of those standing there, such as will never taste death until they see the sovereignty of God." 28Yet it happened after these words [about eight days], taking Rock and Yochanan and Ya'aqov he ascended into the mountain to pray. 29And it happened while he prayed the appearance of his face was different and his garments flashed out white. 30And look: two men were speaking together with him, such as were Mosheh and Eliyah, 31who were seen in glory speaking of his exodus which he was about to fulfill in Yerushalem. 32Yet Rock and those with him were weighed down with sleep. But becoming alert, they saw his glory and the two men standing with him. 33And it happened as they were being separated from him, Rock said to Yeshua, "Master, it is good for us to be here, and we shall build three lodges: one yours and one Mosheh's and one Eliyah's." [Not knowing what he was saying.] 34But while he was saying this there came a cloud and overshadowed them, and they were afraid when they entered into the cloud. 35And there came a voice from the cloud, saying, "This is my son, the chosen: him hear." 36And when the voice came, Yeshua was found alone.

In this heavenly vision two figures of Rabbinic tradition who were understood not to have tasted death, Moses and Elijah, also make their appearance. Elijah, of course, is the primordial prophet of the Merkabah. Elijah's *talmid*, Elisha, sees Elijah taken up into the heavens and God's "chariot of fire and horses of fire" (2 Kings 2:11). [The term for "chariot" here is *rekhev*, simply the masculine form of the feminine Merkabah.] At least from the time of Josephus, Moses was also held to have been taken up alive into the heavenly court.[19] Taken together, then, Elijah and Moses are indices of Jesus' access to the heavenly court. Peter's apparently inept suggestion to his rabbi of building "lodges" also corresponds to the enclosure for God's glory on earth which Moses is commanded to build in the chapters of Exodus after chapter 24. Taken as a whole, the Transfiguration at its generative moment attests Jesus' introduction of his *talmidim* to a vision of the divine throne comparable to his own at his baptism.

Jesus' conscious framing of a *kabbalah*, an approach to the divine Merkabah for himself and for his own *talmidim*, naturally includes an understanding of his own identity. Who is it that can offer this approach? Luke's presentation of what Jesus had to say in a synagogue at Nazareth, the first village he knew, provides a precise indication of just this self-consciousness. Luke's Gospel also presents a clear-eyed profile of Jesus as Messiah by means of reference to the book of Isaiah, as we shall see. Throughout, Luke prepares us for the meaning of Jesus' messianic status by a fairly straightforward enhancement of an element in the commonly Synoptic account of Jesus' baptism. All three Synoptics have Jesus propelled by the Spirit into the wilderness, in order to be pressed to the limit by Satan (Matt. 4:1; Mark 1:12; Luke 4:1), and Matthew and Luke both include three itemized temptations at this point (Matt. 4:1–11; Luke 4:1–13). In all three, the sense is conveyed that one's possession of the Spirit of God in baptism brings one into conflict with the primordial source of resistance to that Spirit. But Luke's articulation of that necessary resistance to the Spirit is the most fulsome and explicit (Luke 4:1–2):

> [1]But Yeshua, full of Holy Spirit, returned from the Yordan, and was being led by the Spirit in the wilderness [2]forty days, pressed to the limit by the devil.

The repeated reference to the Spirit here makes all the more emphatic the uniquely Lukan insistence that Jesus was "full of Holy Spirit," and

---

19. See *Antiquities* 4 §326. For further discussion, see Chilton, "The Transfiguration: Dominical Assurance and Apostolic Vision," *New Testament Studies* 27 (1980) 115–124.

that expression proves to be key in the unfolding motifs of this section of the Gospel.

Again, after the story of his temptations,[20] Luke alone has Jesus return "in the power of the Spirit into Galilee" (Luke 4:14). There can be no question, then, that at this paradigmatic moment, as Jesus commences his public activity, the issue of the Spirit is uppermost in the reference to Jesus' divine identity within Luke. The inauguration of this activity takes place — only in Luke — by means of an appearance in a synagogue in Nazareth, where his citation of the book of Isaiah is pivotal (Luke 4:14–30):

> [14]And Yeshua returned in the power of the Spirit into Galilaia. And news went out into all the surrounding land concerning him. [15]He himself was teaching in their synagogues and was glorified by all. [16]And he came into Nazeret, where he had been nurtured, and he entered according to his custom on the day of the Shabbat into the synagogue. [17]And he arose to read and there was delivered to him a book, of the prophet Yeshayah. He opened the book and found the place where it was written, [18]"The Lord's Spirit is upon me, forasmuch as he anointed me to message triumph to the poor. He delegated me to proclaim release to captives and recovery of sight to the blind, to dispatch the broken with release, [19]to proclaim an acceptable year of the Lord!" [20]He rolled the book, gave it back to the assistant, and sat. And of all, the eyes in the congregation were staring at him. [21]But he began to say to them that: "Today this scripture has been fulfilled in your ears!" [22]And all attested him and marveled at the words of grace that proceeded out from his mouth, and they were saying, "Is he not Yosef's son?" [23]And he said to them, "You will by all means say this comparison to me, 'Physician, heal yourself!' As much as we heard happened in Kafar-Nachum, do also here, in your own country!" [24]But he said, "Amen I say to you that no prophet is acceptable in his own country. [25]Yet in truth I say to you, there were many widows in Eliyah's days in Yisra'el, when the heaven was shut three years and six months, as a great famine came on all the earth, [26]and to none of them was Eliyah sent, except to Zarafta of Sidonia, to a widow woman. [27]And there were many scabby people in Yisra'el while Elisha was prophet, and

---

20. The story of itemized temptations is the contribution of the source called "Q;" for an account of the contents of "Q," cf. Chilton, *Pure Kingdom. Jesus' Vision of God: Studying the Historical Jesus 1* (Eerdmans: Grand Rapids and London: SPCK, 1996) 107–110.

none of them was cleansed, except Na'aman the Syrian." [28]And all in the synagogue were filled with rage when they heard this; [29]they arose and threw him outside of the city and led him to an edge of the mount on which the city was built, so as to hurl him down. [30]But he went through their midst and proceeded.

A great deal in this passage models the ideal activity within synagogues and worship more generally which both Luke and Acts portray, but the focus on the Spirit is the crux of the whole.

The utility of this passage with the overall structure of Luke-Acts has led to the finding that it has been synthesized by the editorial work which went into those two documents. And the utility of the passage within Luke-Acts cannot reasonably be denied. The entire pericope, from v. 14 until v. 30 in Luke 4, sets up a model — of reading scripture in a synagogue, enjoying some success but then violent rejection, a rejection that leads to a turning to non-Jews — which corresponds to the experience of Paul and Barnabas in the book of Acts, especially at Pisidian Antioch (that is, Antioch in Asia Minor, not on the Orontes) in Acts 13:13–52.[21] Together, Luke 4 and Acts 13 set out a pattern for the Church of Luke-Acts. The name "Antioch" is a key to the importance of the latter passage, just as the verb "to anoint" in the former passage is profoundly evocative. The two are as if violins in an orchestra set at a quaver distance, at which one instrument causes the other to resonate. For Luke-Acts, Paul and Barnabas resonate with the purpose, program and authorization of Jesus himself.

The words cited from Isaiah begin, "The Lord's Spirit is upon me, forasmuch as he anointed me." Here, then, is the specification of how the Spirit has been with Jesus since the moment of his baptism. The Spirit is his anointing. In Greek, as in Hebrew and Aramaic, the term "Messiah" means most basically "anointed one." This etymology is of more than academic interest, because the very verb used here (*khrio*) associated itself in the ear of a Greek-speaker with the term "Messiah" or "Christ" (*khristos*). Jesus is Messiah because the Spirit is upon him, and the text from Isaiah becomes an itinerary of his activity.

Just here, however, the dissonance between Jesus' own typical activity and the text of Isaiah 61, cited by Luke, becomes evident. The simple facts are that Isa. 61:1–2 refers to things Jesus never did, such as re-

---

21. I have worked out this correspondence in some detail in *God in Strength: Jesus' Announcement of the Kingdom*, Studien zum Neuen Testament und seiner Umwelt 1 (Freistadt: Plöchl, 1979) 123–156.

leasing prisoners from jail, and that Jesus did things the text makes no mention of, such as declaring people free of impurity (see Matt. 8:2–4; Mark 1:40–45; Luke 5:12–16). This dissonance is not a Lukan creation, because the pattern of the Gospel is to make the correspondence to the Septuagint in biblical citations as close as possible. As the text stands, moreover, a change from any known form of the biblical text results in a lost opportunity to relate directly to the activity of Jesus, as well as introducing an element of greater dissonance. The phrase "to bind the broken of heart" is omitted from the citation, and wording similar to Isa. 58:6, a reference to setting the oppressed at liberty, has been inserted.

Although Luke's Gospel presents the wording — evidently inspired from Isaiah — as a routine reading in a synagogue, it evidently was not so in the tradition prior to Luke. Jesus' "citation" is no citation at all, but a freer version of the biblical book than could have been read. The wording of the passage in the Old Syriac Gospels (in a language closely related to Jesus' indigenous Aramaic) is freer still:

The Spirit of the Lord is upon *you*,
on account of which he has anointed *you* to message triumph to
the poor;
And he has sent *me* to preach to the captives release, and to the
blind sight
— and *I* will free the broken with release —
and to preach the acceptable year of the Lord.

The oddities Luke preserves are present, together with what has been homogenized in Luke: the radical change in pronouns.[22] By speaking these words, Jesus portrays himself as responding to a divine charge: "The Spirit of the Lord is upon you, on account of which he has anointed you to message triumph to the poor." Then he emphatically accepts that charge: "And he has sent me to preach to the captives release, and to the blind sight — and I will free the broken with release — and to preach the acceptable year of the Lord." Both the charge and the emphatic acceptance are produced by the signal changes in pronouns, which are italicized above. They are part and parcel of a conscious alteration of the language taken from the book of Isaiah, an alteration which voices the text in a way that makes it akin to the baptismal *bath qol* and the *bath qol* at the Transfiguration.

---

22. For a full discussion, see Chilton, *God in Strength: Jesus' Announcement of the Kingdom,* Studien zum Neuen Testament und seiner Umwelt 1 (Freistadt: Plöchl, 1979) 157–177.

The alteration is typical of Jesus' style of employing Scripture, espe-cially the book of Isaiah (and especially in a targumic form).[23] His aim was to use the Scripture as a lens of his own activity of behalf of God, such that the wording focused on how God was active in what he said and did, without suggesting a complete fit between the text and what Jesus referred to. The Scripture was a guide to the experience of God in the present, but that experience was more important than the text and could be used to refashion the text. This passage from Luke brings us to the wellspring of Jesus' understanding of himself in messianic terms. He declared that his anointing with the Spirit of God empowered and constrained him to act on God's behalf.

Scholarship has been deflected from a due appreciation of this pas-sage. The identification of Jesus as Messiah has been freighted with the assumption that the term "Messiah" must be understood with a specific political, priestly, and/or prophetic meaning in order to be employed. Because Jesus cannot be associated directly with any such program, it is routinely denied that Jesus applied the term to himself.[24] Clearly, the association of Jesus as Messiah with the Spirit gained currency after and as a consequence of the resurrection, as we have already seen. But its currency is very difficult to explain, as Marinus de Jonge points out, if "Jesus himself avoided this designation and discouraged his follow-ers from using it."[25] Some consistent usage of messianic language would likely have been in the background of Jesus' teaching for the term to have emerged as the primary designation of Jesus. In that Luke's Gospel was composed in Antioch around 90 c.e. in a community in which both Greek and Aramaic were spoken, it is the most likely source among the Synoptics to have indicated what this background may have been. The tight connection between the Spirit of God and the verb "anoint," as in Jesus' reference to Isaiah 61 in Luke 4, provides us with just the indi-cation which fills out the picture of the development of early Christian usage. Anointed by the Spirit of God, Jesus viewed himself as enacting and articulating the claims of God's sovereignty ("the kingdom of God"). His teaching indeed does not spell out the content of being "Messiah" by means of a precise program drawn from biblical or pseudepigraphic

---

23. See Chilton, A Galilean Rabbi and His Bible. Jesus' Use of the Interpreted Scripture of His Time (Wilmington: Glazier, 1984), also published with the subtitle, Jesus' Own Interpretation of Isaiah (London: SPCK, 1984).

24. See Marinus de Jonge, Early Christology and Jesus' Own View of His Mission: Studying the Historical Jesus (Grand Rapids: Eerdmans, 1998) 98–106 for a cautious and skeptical assessment of this denial.

25. De Jonge, 101.

literature, but it does relate the Spirit to his own activity, and in Luke 4 that relationship involves explicitly messianic language.

But the Lukan presentation is precisely what makes the form of the "citation" of Isaiah 61 all the more surprising. As a Lukan invention, the reference would have accorded with the Septuagint. Indeed, the Old Syriac Gospels provide an insight into the shape of the reference to Isaiah 61 by Jesus before it was partially accommodated to the Septuagint within the Lukan presentation. The fractured reference to Isaiah 61 focuses Jesus' messianic identity on the issue of the Spirit, and that was the point of departure for the development of primitive Christian messiology, and therefore of christology in the proper sense.

Luke provides us with a centered view of Jesus' christology, focused on the Spirit of God. Within the recent study of Jesus, two discarded pictures of his christology have emerged again, and I would suggest in closing that they are likely to be discarded again. The first stresses the undoubted importance of the political challenge to the identity of Israel within the first century. Jesus then becomes the "Davidic Messiah," a ruling figure who sets up his throne in association with the Temple.[26] This, despite the portrayal of Jesus in the Temptations as rejecting a picture of such rule, and despite his own rhetorical question, "How do the scribes say the Messiah is David's son?" (Mark 12:35, together with Matt. 22:42; Luke 20:41). That question assumes a tradition of identifying the Messiah and the *ben David*, but it also — and obviously — refutes it.[27] Any messianic theology inherently involved a political dimension, but to make that dimension the only index of meaning runs against the grain of Jesus' contention that Davidic and messianic claims were not simply identifiable. Another view, derived ultimately from Albert Schweitzer's picture of Jesus as a failed apocalyptist, imagines Jesus as personally taking on himself all the conditions of the covenant with Israel, in a desperate attempt to get God to fulfill the covenantal promises.[28] This, despite the fact that the term "covenant" within sayings of Jesus only appears in a single case, in what seems to be a liturgical addition to the meaning of the cup of wine in the context of his last meals in Jerusalem.[29] Peter and Paul were undoubtedly

---

26. For a sophisticated argument to this effect, see Richard A. Horsley, *Sociology and the Jesus Movement* (New York: Crossroad, 1989) 105–145.

27. See Chilton, "Jesus ben David: Reflections on the *Davidssohnfrage*," *Journal for the Study of the New Testament* 14 (1982) 88–112.

28. For this neo-orthodox re-reading of Schweitzer, see N. T. Wright, *Jesus and the Victory of God* (Minneapolis: Fortress, 1993).

29. For a full discussion, see Chilton, *A Feast of Meanings. Eucharistic Theologies from Jesus through Johannine Circles: Supplements to Novum Testamentum* 72 (Leiden: Brill, 1994) 75–92.

theologians of this covenant, because they had directly to face the issues of who was and was not of the people of God. Jesus, however, does not appear to have confronted that question in covenantal terms.

But once Jesus' approach to the Merkabah, on the basis of his endowment with Spirit, is seen to be the pivot of his experience and his program of activity, his care in defining how he was and how he was not Messiah acquires its sense. His messianic identity was a function of his self-consciousness and the awareness of his *talmidim* that his *kabbalah* offers the vision of God in his glory because divine Spirit makes that vision possible.

THREE

The Sage's Good Death

When R. Eliezer fell ill, his disciples came in to pay a call on him. They said to him, "Our master, teach us the ways of life, so that through them we may merit the world to come."

He said to them, "Be attentive to the honor owing to your fellows, keep your children from excessive reflection and set them among the knees of disciples of sages, and when you pray, know before whom you stand, and on that account you will merit the life of the world to come."

And when R. Yohanan ben Zakkai fell ill, his disciples came in to pay a call on him. When he saw them, he began to cry. His disciples said to him, "Light of Israel! Pillar at the right hand! Mighty hammer! On what account are you crying?"

He said to them, "If I were going to be brought before a mortal king, who is here today and tomorrow gone to the grave, who, should he be angry with me, will not be angry forever, and if he should imprison me, will not imprison me forever, and if he should put me to death, whose sentence of death is not for eternity, and whom I can appease with the right words or bribe with money, even so, I should weep.

"But now that I am being brought before the King of kings of kings, the Holy One, blessed be He, who endures forever and ever, who, should he be angry with me, will be angry forever, and if he should imprison me, will imprison me forever, and if he should put me to death, whose sentence of death is for eternity, and whom I cannot appease with the right words or bribe with money, "and not only so, but before me are two paths, one to the Garden of Eden and the other to Gehenna, and I do not know by which path I shall be brought, and should I not weep?"

They said to him, "Our master, bless us."

He said to them, "May it be God's will that the fear of Heaven be upon you as much as the fear of mortal man."

His disciples said, "Just so much?"

He said to them, "Would that it were that much. You should know that, when a person commits a transgression, he says, 'I hope no one sees me.'"

When he was dying, he said to them, "Clear out utensils from the house, because of the uncleanness [of the corpse, which I am about to impart when I die], and prepare a throne for Hezekiah king of Judah, who is coming."

— BAVLI-TRACTATE BERAKHOT 4:2 I:2/28A

Yohanan died in full command of his senses, entirely aware of the next step in his life. Exemplifying a good death, he expressed his humility before the judgment that awaited. As he lay dying, no sage represented in the classical writings of Judaism cited Ps. 22:1, "My God, my God, why hast thou forsaken me?" But if they died serenely, it was not with an excess of self-confidence or pride. For, with all humanity, all of them expected to come before God in judgment, and none took vindication for granted. Death takes place in the context of faith, and the spirituality of Judaism comes to concrete embodiment in that larger context as well. For sages and the Torah that they shaped for all of holy Israel, not only did death form a natural stage in human life, but it also marked a step on a longer journey, one that led to eternal life. So how sages described the good death makes sense within the conviction, critical to Judaism, that humanity can vanquish death and attain life eternal. Rabban Yohanan's last lesson to his disciples tells the tale: "I am going before an honest judge, who will decide my fate for eternity." Even a life spent in study and teaching of the Torah, a life lived in the presence of God, contained within it its share of arrogant sinfulness, and Yohanan did not take for granted God's favor, let alone God's grace. That constituted his final Torah-teaching: "Fear God as much as you fear people."

Certainly the exemplary figure of those who fear God as much as they fear people is Moses, whom sages know as "our rabbi." It is fitting that this account of the good death should both begin and end with the figure of Moses, especially since the Rabbinic writings provide two pictures of how Moses died, each with its lesson. One is as follows:

At that moment the Holy One, blessed be He, said to the angel of death, "Go, bring me the soul of Moses."

He went and stood before him and said to him, "Moses, give me your soul.'"

He said to him, "In a place in which I am in session, you have no right to stand, and yet you say to me, 'Give me your soul?'" He growled at him and the other went forth in a huff.

The angel of death went and brought the tale back to the Omnipotent. Once again the Holy One, blessed be He, said to the angel of death, "Go, bring me the soul of Moses."

He went to where he was and looked for him but did not find him.

He went to the sea and said to it, "As to Moses, have you seen him?"

The sea said to him, "From the day on which he brought Israel through my midst, I have not seen him."

He went to the mountains and said to them, "As to Moses, have you seen him?"

They said to him, "From the day on which the Israelites received the Torah on Mount Sinai, we have not seen him."

He went to Gehenna and said to it, "As to Moses, have you seen him?"

It said to him, "I have heard his name, but him I have never seen."

He went to the ministering angels and said to them, "As to Moses, have you seen him?"

They said to him, "Go to mortals."

He went to Israel and said to them, "As to Moses, have you seen him?"

They said to him, "God knows his way. God has hidden him away for the life of the world to come, and no creature knows where he is."

For it is said, "And he was buried in the valley" (Deut. 34:6).

When Moses died, Joshua wept, crying out and mourning for him bitterly.

He said, "My father, my father, my lord, my lord.

"My father, for he raised me, my lord, for he taught me Torah."

And he mourned for him for many days, until the Holy One, blessed be He, said to Joshua, "Joshua, how long are you going to continue this mourning of yours? And has Moses died only unto you alone? And has he not died, also, unto me? For from the moment that he died, there has been deep mourning before me, as it is said,

'And in that day did the Lord, God of hosts, call to weeping and to lamentation' (Isa. 22:12). But it is certain for him that he gains the world to come, as it is said, 'And the Lord said to Moses, Behold, you are going to sleep with your fathers and...will arise' (Deut. 31:16)."

— Sifré to Deuteronomy CCCV:III

The angel of death cannot prevail over the Torah, a point we shall meet again. All of nature conspired against death. But Moses died, and Joshua wept — not for Moses, but for himself. Death affects the living; that is who mourns. But Joshua and God both take comfort from the fact that Moses certainly will enter the world to come — a fitting contrast to the uncertainty on that same matter that Yohanan ben Zakkai expresses, a mark of the humility of the sage.

The sages of the Oral Torah exemplify a good death. What this means at its essential point is simple: The Torah calls on humanity to exercise free will by obeying God's Torah, and sin results from arrogance, virtue from humility. The story of the human condition, from the creation of Man and Woman forward, is the tale of the struggle between the passionate, commanding God, who has created humanity, and within humanity, Israel, and endowed them with the freedom to obey and love God or to disobey and defy God. How this plays itself out in connection with the death of sages presents no surprises: the great sage dies at a moment of humility before God, on the one side, and of Torah-study, on the other. The good death makes a statement of humility.

Given sages' conviction that humanity was made to study the Torah, we may hardly find surprising that the good death encompassed Torah-study, as in the case of Yohanan ben Zakkai. His mind to the very end focused upon what his disciples could and should learn from him, even at the hour of his death. Now to exemplify the good death — the death in the midst of Torah-study — we come now to the stories about the death of a sage, with special reference to Eliezer ben Hyrcanus. The death-scene we consider responds to lists of omens pertinent to one's condition at death:

Ben Azzai says, "Whoever has a serene mind on account of his learning has a good omen for himself, and who does not have a serene mind on account of his learning has a bad omen for himself. Whoever has a serene mind on account of his impulse, has a good omen for himself, but if his mind is distressed because of his impulse, it is a bad sign for him. For him with whom the sages are satisfied

at the hour of death it is a good sign, and for him with whom sages
are not satisfied at the hour of death it is a bad sign. For whoever
has his face turned upward [at death] it is a good sign, and for
whoever has his face turned toward the bed it is a bad sign. If one
is looking at people, it is a good sign, at the wall, a bad sign. If one's
face is glistening, it is a good sign, glowering, a bad one."

— The Fathers according to Rabbi Nathan XXV:I.I

[Ben Azzai] would say, "If one dies in a serene mind, it is a good
omen from him, in derangement, it is a bad omen . . . while speaking, it is a good omen, in silence, a bad omen . . . in repeating words
of the Torah, it is a good omen for him, in the midst of discussing
business, it is a bad omen . . . while doing a religious duty, it is a good
omen, while involved with a trivial matter, it is a bad omen . . . while
happy, it is a good omen, while sad, a bad omen . . . while laughing,
a good omen, while weeping, a bad omen . . . on the eve of the Sabbath, a good omen, at the end of the Sabbath, a bad omen . . . on
the eve of the Day of Atonement a bad omen, at the end of the
Day of Atonement a good omen."

— The Fathers according to Rabbi Nathan XXV:III:I

Ben Azzai's statement weaves the theme of dying into the tapestry of
Torah-study. Yohanan has shown us what it means to die while repeating
words of Torah, doing a religious duty — Torah-study. Certainly the most
elaborate account of how a sage dies carries us to the death-bed of Eliezer
ben Hyrcanus. The rabbinic writings accord him — and Aqiba, as we
shall see in Chapter Five — with an account of beginning and ending.
We now have an elaborate story illustrating how a great sage dies:

When Rabbi Eliezer was dying — they say it was the eve of the
Sabbath [toward dusk] [thus: " . . . on the eve of the Sabbath, a
good omen"] — R. Aqiba and his colleagues came in to see him,
and he was dozing in the room, sitting back on a canopied couch.
They took seats in the waiting room. Hyrcanus his son came in to
remove his phylacteries [which are worn on week days but not on
the Sabbath, about to begin]. But he did not let him do so, and he
was weeping.

Hyrcanus went out and said to the sages, "My lords, it appears
to me that my father is deranged."

[Eliezer] said to him, "My son, I am not the one who is deranged,
but you are the one who is deranged. For you have neglected to

light the lamp for the Sabbath, on which account you may become liable to the death penalty inflicted by heaven ["...while doing a religious duty, it is a good omen, while involved with a trivial matter, it is a bad omen"], but busied yourself with the matter of the phylacteries, on account of which liability is incurred, at worst, merely on the matter of violating the rules of Sabbath rest."

Since sages saw that he was in full command of his faculties, they came in and took up seats before him [to engage in Torah-study] ["...in repeating words of the Torah, it is a good omen for him, in the midst of discussing business, it is a bad omen"], but at a distance of four cubits [as was required, because Eliezer was in a state of ostracism on account of his rejection of the decision of the majority in a disputed case]. [Bringing up the case subject to dispute, so to determine whether he had finally receded to the decision of the majority,] they said to him, "My lord, as to a round cushion, a ball, [a shoe when placed on] a shoemaker's last, an amulet, and phylacteries that have been torn, what is the law as to their being susceptible to uncleanness? [Are they regarded as completed and useful objects, therefore susceptible, or are they classified as useless or incomplete and therefore not susceptible?]"

[Maintaining his earlier position, for which he had been ostracized or placed in excommunication] he said to them, "They remain susceptible to uncleanness, and should they become unclean, immerse them as is [without undoing them, e.g., exposing their contents to the water], and take great pains in these matters, for these represent important laws that were stated to Moses at Sinai."

They persisted in addressing to him questions concerning matters of insusceptibility and susceptibility to uncleanness as well as concerning immersion-pools, saying to him, "My lord, what is the rule on this matter?"

He would say to them, "Clean."

And so he went, giving the answer of susceptible to uncleanness to an object that could become unclean, and insusceptible to one that could not become unclean ["If one dies in a serene mind, it is a good omen from him, in derangement, it is a bad omen"].

The mark of the sage is that, at the hour of death, he continues to engage in study of the Torah. The blessing that the sage receives is that he is able to do so even to his last breath. But the story proceeds to a new chapter: Eliezer points to the ostracism that has kept at a distance the disciples of the generation he served as a sage:

> After a while Rabbi Eliezer said to sages, "I am amazed at the disciples of the generation, perhaps they may are liable to the death penalty at the hand of Heaven."
>
> They said to him, "My lord, on what account?"
>
> He said to them, "Because you never came and performed the work of apprenticeship to me."
>
> Then he said to Aqiba ben Joseph, "Aqiba, on what account did you not come before me and serve as apprentice to me?"
>
> He said to him, "My lord, I had no time."
>
> He said to him, "I shall be surprised for you if you die a natural death."
>
> And some say, He said nothing to him, but when Rabbi Eliezer spoke as he did to his disciples, forthwith [Aqiba's] heart melted within him.
>
> Said to him Rabbi Aqiba, "My lord, how will I die?"
>
> He said to him, "Aqiba, yours will be the worst."

Now commences the last Torah-lesson:

> Rabbi Aqiba entered and took a seat before him and said to him, "My lord, now repeat traditions for me."
>
> He opened a subject and repeated for him three hundred rules concerning the bright spot [to which Lev. 13:1ff. refers in connection with the skin ailment translated as leprosy].
>
> Then Rabbi Eliezer raised his two arms and folded them on his breast and said, "Woe is me for these two arms, which are like two scrolls of Torahs, which now are departing from the world. For were all the oceans ink, all the reeds quills, all men scribes, they could not write down what I have learned in Scripture and repeated in Mishnah-traditions, and derived as lessons from my apprenticeship to sages in the session. Yet I have taken away from my masters only as much as does a person who dips his finger into the ocean, and I have taken away for my disciples only so much as a paintbrush takes from a paint tube. And furthermore, I can repeat three hundred laws on the rule: '*You shall not permit a sorceress to live.*'
>
> "But no one ever asked me anything about it, except for Aqiba ben Joseph.

"For one time he said to me, 'My lord, teach me how people plant cucumbers and how they pull them up.' I said something and the entire field was filled with cucumbers.

"He said to me, 'My lord, you have taught me how they are planted. Teach me how they are pulled up.' I said something, and all of the cucumbers assembled in a single place."

Now we address those controversial, if trivial, matters of law for the sake of which Eliezer accepted excommunication for much of his active life as a master of the Torah:

> Said Rabbi Eleazar ben Azariah to him, "My lord, as to a shoe that is on the shoemaker's list, what is the law? [Is it susceptible to uncleanness, as a useful object, or insusceptible, since it is not fully manufactured and so finished as a useful object?]"
>
> He said to him, "It is insusceptible to uncleanness."
>
> And so he continued giving answers to questions, ruling of an object susceptible to uncleanness that it is susceptible, and of one insusceptible to uncleanness that it is permanently clean, until his soul went forth as he said the word, "Clean."
>
> Then Rabbi Eleazar ben Azariah tore his clothes and wept, going forth and announcing to sages, "My lords, come and see Rabbi Eliezer, for he is not in a state of purity as to the world to come, since his soul went forth with the word pure on his lips."
>
> After the Sabbath Rabbi Aqiba came and found [Eliezer's corpse being conveyed for burial] on the road from Caesarea to Lud. Then he tore his clothes and ripped his hair, and his blood flowed, and he fell to the earth, crying out and weeping, saying, "Woe is me for you, my Lord, woe is me, my master, for you have left the entire generation orphaned."
>
> At the row of mourners he commenced [the lament,] saying, *"My father, my father, chariot of Israel and its horsemen!* I have coins but no expert money-changer to sort them out."
>
> — The Fathers according to Rabbi Nathan XXV:IV.1–5

The story serves as a good illustration for three of the positive omens Ben Azzai has listed, while speaking, while repeating words of the Torah, and on the eve of the Sabbath. But he clearly is not represented as happy or cheerful or laughing, so, in the aggregate, I think that an illustration of the omens of Ben Azzai form a negligible consideration in the mind of the storytellers. The center of interest of the story is Eliezer's complaint against the disciples, who did not study Torah through service to him. But for our purposes, the point is other. It is to underscore that, to the very end, the sage engages in Torah-study and its issues — as though death were not present at all.

Why should death on its own have played so slight a role in the accounts of the sages' deaths? What did Yohanan mean when he spoke of a path to the Garden of Eden? Let us start back with sages' thinking about death. And to understand that thought, we must begin with their convictions about what life requires — "If you have learned much Torah, do not puff yourself up on that account, for it was for that purpose that you were created" — and the place of death within life.

> When he goes in [to the study hall], what does [the disciple] say?
> "May it please you, Lord my God, that no mishap will occur on my account [Mishnah-tractate Berakhot 4:2C], that I not err in a matter of law, that my colleagues may rejoice in me, that I may not call something unclean clean or something clean unclean, that my colleagues not err in a matter of law, and that I may take pleasure in them."
>
> When he goes out, what does he say?
>
> "I thank you, Lord my God, that you have set my portion among those who sit in the school house and have not set my portion among those who sit idly on street corners. For I get up in the morning and they get up in the morning. I get up to words of Torah, and they get up to nonsense. I work and they work. I work and receive a reward, and they work and do not receive a reward. I run and they run. I run to the life of the world to come, and they run to the pit of destruction."
>
> — Bavli-tractate Berakhot 4:2 I:1/28A

The measure of pride that characterizes the prayer diminishes when we remember Yohanan ben Zakkai's humility, after a life of Torah-study. The disciple of the sage has the right to thank God for the portion that God has meted out, a life of penury and even separation from loved ones perhaps, but also a life that produces a reward for work, meaning, life of the world to come.

The sage sets forth the model of the good death, which is to say, death in full consciousness of what is happening, rich in hope for what is going to happen: "I run to the life of the world to come." As a matter of fact, the natural course of life, to seventy or even eighty years, represents how God made us and what God wants for us:

Hama bar Hanina and Rabbi Jonathan:

Hama bar Hanina said, "The first human being (Adam) was worthy not to have to taste the taste of death. And why was the penalty of death applied to him? The Holy One, blessed be He, foresaw that Nebuchadnezzar and Hiram were destined to turn themselves into gods. Therefore the penalty of having to die was imposed upon humanity. That is in line with this verse of Scripture: 'You were in Eden, the garden of God' (Ezek. 28:13). And was Hiram actually in Eden? But he said to him, 'You are the one who caused that one in Eden to have to die.'"

Hama's simple logic builds upon the fact that God planned for humanity to live eternally, but the sin of Man and Woman brought death into the world. But Man and Woman can regain the Garden of Eden and so enter life eternal, overcoming the grave. This would take place after judgment. To that view Jonathan objects:

Said Rabbi Jonathan to him, "If so, God should have decreed death only for the wicked, but not for the righteous. Rather, it was so that the wicked should not be able hypocritically to pretend to repent, so that they should not have occasion to say, 'Are not the righteous living on and on? It is only because they form a treasure of merit accruing on account of the practice of doing religious duties as well as good deeds. We too shall lay up a treasure of merit accruing from doing religious duties and good deeds.' What would come out is that the things they do would not be done sincerely [for their own sake, but only for the sake of gaining merit]. [That is what is good about death. It prevents the wicked from perverting the holy life by doing the right thing for the wrong reason. Everyone dies, so there is no point in doing religious duties only so as to avoid dying.]"

The next passage makes explicit the matter of judgment of the righteous. They too have to struggle against the impulse to do evil, and when they die, the judgment of Heaven weighs their deeds, good and wicked. When they come close to balancing (as they do for most people), God then inclines the balance toward justification, and they regain eternal life in Eden:

Rabbi Yohanan and Rabbit Simeon ben Laqish:

Rabbi Yohanan said, "On what account was a decree of death issued against the wicked? It is because, so long as the wicked live, they anger the Holy One, blessed be He. That is in line with the following verse of Scripture: 'You have wearied the Lord with your deeds' (Mal. 2:17). When they die, they stop angering the Holy One, blessed be He. That is in line with the following verse of Scripture: 'There the wicked cease from raging' (Job 3:17). There the wicked cease angering the Holy One, blessed be He.

"On what account, however, is the decree of death issued against the righteous? It is because so long as the righteous live, they have to conduct warfare against their impulse to do evil. When they die, they find rest. That is in line with this verse: 'And there the weary are at rest' (Job 3:17). 'It is enough, we have labored long enough.'"

Simeon ben Laqish said, "It is so as to give an ample reward for the one, and to exact ample punishment from the other. To give ample reward to the righteous, who really never were worthy of having to taste the taste of death, but accepted the taste of death for themselves. Therefore: 'in their land they shall possess double' (Isa. 61:7). 'And to exact ample punishment from the wicked,' for the righteous had not been worthy of having to taste the taste of death, but they had accepted the taste of death for themselves on account [of the wicked]. Therefore: 'And destroy them with a double destruction' (Jer. 17:18)."

— GENESIS RABBAH IX:V.1–3

Through life, the righteous struggle against their impulse to do evil; death ends the struggle and opens the way to a life of peace and contentment. For this Judaism maintains that when we die, we go on to "the world to come," "the Garden of Eden," "the Heavenly academy," or, in the other direction, to Gehenna, but only for a spell. That is until the Messiah comes to announce that the dead are to be raised. Then comes the last judgment, at which the fate of all humanity — everyone who ever lived — is settled.

A variety of sayings and stories in the oral Torah clarify sages' view of the fate of the soul after death. Souls retain consciousness and can even communicate with the living.

Rabbi Hiyya and Rabbi Jonathan were discoursing while walking in a cemetery. The blue fringes [of the show-fringes] of Rabbi Jonathan were trailing on the ground. Said Rabbi Hiyya to him, "Lift them up, so that [the dead] should not say, 'Tomorrow they are coming to us, and now they are ridiculing us.'"

He said to him, "Do the dead know so much as that? And lo, it is written, 'But the dead do not know a thing' (Qoh. 9:5)."

He said to him, "If you have studied Scripture, you have not reviewed what you learned, and if you reviewed what you learned, you failed to do it a third time, and if you did it a third time, then people did not explain the meaning to you. 'For the living know that they shall die' (Qoh. 9:5) refers to the righteous, for, when they have died, they still are called the living. 'But the dead know nothing:' This refers to the wicked, who, even while they are alive, are called dead, as it is said, 'And you, wicked one, who are slain, the prince of Israel' (Ezek. 21:30)."

> — Talmud of Babylonia tractate Berakhot 18a–b

The righteous, when they die, continue to know what happens in the world, but the wicked perish and lose all consciousness. Communication with the dead takes place so that, under certain circumstances, the living may call up the dead and address questions to them:

The father of Samuel held some money for an estate. When he died, Samuel was not with him [so he did not know where the money was]. People called him, "The son of someone who robs estates." Samuel came after [his father] to the cemetery. He said to them, "I want father."

They said to him, "There are lots of fathers here."

He said to them, "I want father, son of father."

They said to him, "There are lots of fathers, sons of fathers, here too."

He said to them, "I want father, son of father, the father of Samuel. Where is he?"

They said to him, "He has gone up to the academy in the firmament."

In the meantime he saw Levi, who was seated outside [away from the rest of the deceased].

He said to him, "Why are you seated outside? Why did you not go up?"

He said to him, "They told me that for as many years as you did not go up to the session of Rabbi Efes and so you injured his feelings, we are not going to take you up to the academy in the firmament."

Meanwhile the father [of Samuel] came along. [Samuel] saw that he was both weeping and smiling. He said, "Why are you weeping?"

He said to him, "Because soon you are coming here."

"Why are you smiling?"

"Because you are highly regarded in this world."

He said to him, "If I am highly regarded, then let them take up Levi." So they took Levi up.

He said to him, "As to the money belonging to the estate, where is it?"

He said to him, "Go and take it out of the case of the millstones. The money at the top and bottom belongs to us, and what is in the middle belongs to the estate."

He said to him, "Why did you do it that way?"

He said to him, "If thieves come, they will steal ours. If the earth rots the money, it will rot ours."

This story again proves that the deceased know what is going on.

But perhaps the case of Samuel is different, since he is highly regarded.

Since that was the case, [in heaven] they went ahead and announced, "Make room for him."

— BABYLONIAN TALMUD TRACTATE BERAKHOT 18B

The upshot is straightforward: death brings to the end the life in this world and opens up the life in the world to come, "This world is like a corridor before the world to come" (Tractate Abot 4:16), and the world to come is the world that is wholly good. But to understand the Judaic doctrine of death as set forth in the classical documents, we must introduce one further consideration, and that is the coming resurrection of the dead at the end of days. That view is stated in so many words in the following:

Rabbi Jacob says, "You have not got a single religious duty that is written in the Torah, the reward of which is not specified alongside, that does not depend for its fulfillment on the resurrection of the dead. For example, with reference to honor of father and mother, it is written, 'That your days may be prolonged and that it may go well with you' (Deut. 5:16); with regard to sending forth the dam out of the nest: 'that it may be well with you and that you may prolong your days' (Deut. 22:6). Now, if someone's father said

to him, 'Climb up into the loft and bring me the pigeons,' and he
went up to the loft, sent away the dam and took the young, and
climbing down, fell and was killed — what are we to make of this
one's 'happiness' and 'length of days'"? But the language, "in order
that it may be well with you" refers to a day that is wholly good;
and "in order that your days may be long" means 'on the day that
is entirely long.'"

— Babylonian Talmud Tractate Qiddushin 39b

Scripture itself, as our sages read it, refers us toward that coming world
of resurrection and eternal life, to which we now turn.

The Torah's doctrine of the fate of the soul after death encompasses
the entirety of sages' religious system, the whole of their thought, beginning with their emphasis upon life in the community of Israel, the
holy people. We do not die alone, but in the context of family, past
and future. And, in the spirituality of Judaism, the Israelite dies within
the framework of Israel as a whole. The fate of the individual forms
a sentence in the chapter that records the tale of holy Israel. Individual life goes forward from this world, past the grave, to the world to
come, and people are both judged and promised eternal life. The two
principal components of the Torah's theology of last things — [1] resurrection and judgment, [2] the world to come and eternal life — take
place in the categorical sequence, individual, then community. What,
exactly, happens after death? First comes the resurrection of individuals
and, with it, judgment of individuals one by one. Then, those chosen
for life having been identified, "the world to come" takes place, and that
final restoration of perfection, involving all Israel in place of Adam, lasts
forever. To be part of Israel is to share in life eternal, and to be Israel
is to accept God's unity and dominion. By that definition, "Israel" forms
the cohort of those chosen for life, and Israelites are restored to life in
the Land of Israel.

Why the stress on resurrection? It is a logical necessity of a theology
revealing God's justice. The sages' Torah insists upon the rationality and
order of the universe under God's rule. Without judgment and eternal life
for the righteous, this world's imbalance — the wicked prosper, the righteous suffer, and bad things happen to good people — cannot be righted,
nor can God's justice be revealed. Monotheism without an eschatology
of judgment and the world to come leaves unresolved the tensions inherent in the starting point: God is one, God is just. That is why the
starting point of the theology dictates its conclusion: the deeds one does

in this world bear consequences for one's situation in the world to come, and the merit attained through this-worldly deeds, e.g., of generosity, persists; individuals retain their status as such through all time to come.

The basic logic of the Torah as sages read it therefore requires the doctrine of personal resurrection, so that the life of this world may go onward to the next. Indeed, without the conception of life beyond the grave the system as a whole yields a mass of contradictions and anomalies: injustice to the righteous, prosperity to the wicked, never recompensed. That explains why, at one point after another, the path to the future passes through, and beyond, the grave and the judgment that, for all Israel with few exceptions, leads to eternity. The principal continues and yields interest, or punishment may take place in this world, while eternal punishment goes onward as well, especially for the trilogy of absolute sins, idolatry, incest (or fornication), and murder, capped by gossip. But how all of this squares with the conception of "all Israel" that transcends individual Israelites remains to be seen.

Now, within that framework, the righteous, who will stand in judgment and enter the world to come, must by definition encompass in their number not only those alive at the very final moment of humanity's life beyond Eden, but also all those who have ever lived. Otherwise where is the order, whence the justice, for the unnumbered ranks of the humble and virtuous who perished in poverty, knowing full well that the arrogant and wicked died after enjoying a long, satisfying, and nasty life? The promise of renewed life, forever, systematically accounted for the ultimate justice of existence, even for private lives. Now, by definition, the world to come cannot commence without the presence of all who belong to the party of life. And that requirement explains why we follow the logical sequence: first, resurrection and judgment, then, the world or the age to come and life eternal. There is no reversing the order, for obvious reasons built into the logic of the theology's basic premise and purpose. Let me state the matter negatively. Only with a complete loss of sense — omission of all those who have died before the end of days — can the world to come and life eternal take place prior to the resurrection of the dead. But then world order proves manifestly unjust. So the very explanation of the justice of world order dictates that matters be just so. In the end of days, accordingly, death will die. The certainty of resurrection derives from a simple fact of restorationist theology: God has already shown that he can do it, so Genesis Rabbah LXXVII:I.1: "You find that everything that the Holy One, blessed be He, is destined to do in the age to come he has already gone ahead and done through the righteous in this world. The Holy One, blessed be He, will raise the dead, and Elijah raised the dead."

Now we come to the specific theological account of the context in which the good death takes place: the resurrection of the dead. What we shall now see is that embodied within the sages' doctrine of how and why we die is their theory of who and what is "Israel," and by "Israel," they mean the holy community that, in this world, stands for, bears witness to God's rule over all humanity. To be Israel means to serve God as God is made manifest in the Torah. The first component of the doctrine of the resurrection of the dead — belief both that the resurrection of the dead will take place _and_ that it is the Torah that reveals that the dead will rise are fundamental to the Oral Torah — is fully exposed in a fundamental composition devoted by the framers of the Mishnah to that subject. The components of the doctrine fit together, in that statement, in a logical order. In a predictable application of the governing principle of measure for measure, those who do not believe in the resurrection of the dead will be punished by being denied what they do not accept. Some few others bear the same fate. But to be Israel means to rise from the grave, and that applies to all Israelites. That is to say, the given of the condition of Israel is that the entire holy people will enter the world to come, which is to say, will enjoy the resurrection of the dead and eternal life. "Israel" then is anticipated to be the people of eternity. Excluded from the category of resurrection and the world to come, then, are only those who by their own sins have denied themselves that benefit. These are those that deny that the teaching of the world to come derives from the Torah, or who deny that the Torah comes from God, or hedonists. Exegesis of Scripture also yields the names of three kings who will not be resurrected, as well as four commoners; also specified generations: the flood, the dispersion, and Sodom, the generation of the wilderness, the party of Korah, and the Ten Tribes:

> All Israelites have a share in the world to come, as it is said, "Your people also shall be all righteous, they shall inherit the land forever; the branch of my planting, the work of my hands, that I may be glorified" (Isa. 60:21).

That single statement serves better than any other to define Israel in the Oral Torah. Now we forthwith take up exceptions:

> And these are the ones who have no portion in the world to come:
> He who says, "The resurrection of the dead is a teaching which

does not derive from the Torah, and the Torah does not come from Heaven; and an Epicurean."

Rabbi Aqiba says, "Also: He who reads in heretical books and he who whispers over a wound and says, 'I will put none of the diseases upon you which I have put on the Egyptians, for I am the Lord who heals you' (Exod. 15:26)."

Abba Saul says, "Also: He who pronounces the divine Name as it is spelled out."

— Mishnah-tractate Sanhedrin 10:1
[Bavli-tractate Sanhedrin 11:1]

From classes of persons, we turn to specified individuals who are denied a place within Israel and entry in the world to come; all but one are Israelites, and the exception, Balaam, has a special relation to Israel, as the gentile prophet who came to curse but ended with a blessing:

Three kings and four ordinary folk have no portion in the world to come.

Three kings: Jeroboam, Ahab, and Manasseh.

Rabbi Judah says, "Manasseh has a portion in the world to come, since it is said, 'And he prayed to him and he was entreated of him and heard his supplication and brought him again to Jerusalem into his kingdom' (2 Chron. 33:13)."

They said to him, "To his kingdom he brought him back, but to the life of the world to come he did not bring him back." Four ordinary folk: Balaam, Doeg, Ahitophel, and Gehazi.

— Mishnah-tractate Sanhedrin 10:2

Then come entire generations of gentiles before Abraham, who might have been considered for eternal life outside of the framework of God's self-manifestation, first to Abraham, then in the Torah. These are the standard sets, the Generation of the Flood, the Generation of the Dispersion, and the Inhabitants of Sodom:

The Generation of the Flood has no share in the world to come, and they shall not stand in the judgment, since it is written, "My spirit shall not judge with man forever" (Gen. 6:3) neither judgment nor spirit.

The Generation of the Dispersion has no share in the world to come, since it is said, "So the Lord scattered them abroad from there upon the face of the whole earth" (Gen. 11:8).

"So the Lord scattered them abroad" — in this world, "and the Lord scattered them from there" — in the world to come.

The inhabitants of Sodom have no portion in the world to come, since it is said, "Now the inhabitants of Sodom were wicked and sinners against the Lord exceedingly" (Gen. 13:13) "Wicked" — "in this world, and sinners" — in the world to come.

But they will stand in judgment. Rabbi Nehemiah says, "Both these and those will not stand in judgment, for it is said, 'Therefore the wicked shall not stand in judgment, nor sinners in the congregation of the righteous' (Ps. 1:5). 'Therefore the wicked shall not stand in judgment' — this refers to the Generation of the Flood. 'Nor sinners in the congregation of the righteous' — this refers to the inhabitants of Sodom."

They said to him, "They will not stand in the congregation of the righteous, but they will stand in the congregation of the sinners."

The spies have no portion in the world to come, as it is said, "Even those who brought up an evil report of the land died by the plague before the Lord" (Num. 14:37) "Died" — in this world. "By the plague" — in the world to come.

— MISHNAH-TRACTATE SANHEDRIN 10:3

What about counterparts in Israel, from the Torah forward? The issue concerns the Generation of the Wilderness, which rejected the Land; the party of Korah; and the Ten Tribes. These match the gentile contingents. But here there is a dispute, and no normative judgment emerges from the Mishnah's treatment of the matter:

"The Generation of the Wilderness has no portion in the world to come and will not stand in judgment, for it is written, 'In this wilderness they shall be consumed and there they shall die' (Num. 14:35)," the words of Rabbi Aqiba.

Rabbi Eliezer says, "Concerning them it says, 'Gather my saints together to me, those that have made a covenant with me by sacrifice' (Ps. 50:5). The party of Korah is not destined to rise up, for it is written, 'And the earth closed upon them' — in this world.

"'And they perished from among the assembly' — in the world to come," the words of Rabbi Aqiba.

And Rabbi Eliezer says, "Concerning them it says, 'The Lord kills and resurrects, brings down to Sheol and brings up again' (1 Sam. 2:6)."

— MISHNAH-TRACTATE SANHEDRIN 10:4

"The Ten Tribes [of northern Israel, exiled by the Assyrians] are not destined to return [with Israel at the time of the resurrection of the dead], since it is said, 'And he cast them into another land, as on this day' (Deut. 29:28). Just as the day passes and does not return, so they have gone their way and will not return," the words of Rabbi Aqiba.

Rabbi Eliezer says, "Just as this day is dark and then grows light, so the Ten Tribes for whom it now is dark — thus in the future it is destined to grow light for them."

— MISHNAH-TRACTATE SANHEDRIN 10:5M

Scripture thus contributes the details that refine the basic proposition; the framer has found the appropriate exclusions. But the prophet, in Scripture, also has provided the basic allegation on which all else rests, that is, "Israel will be entirely righteous and inherit the land forever." Denying the stated dogmas removes a person from the status of "Israel," in line with the opening statement, so to be Israel means to rise from the dead, and Israel as a collectivity is defined as those persons in humanity who are destined to eternal life, a supernatural community.

The resurrection comes to mind whenever death takes an Israelite life, and the monument to the resurrection is the burial ground, the locus of eternity. That is why the coming resurrection of the dead is called to mind whenever one is located in a cemetery:

One who passes between graves [in a cemetery], what does he recite? "Blessed [art Thou, O Lord, our God, King of the Universe,] who resurrects the dead." (Cf. Tosefta Berakhot 6:6.)

Rabbi Hiyya in the name of Rabbi Yohanan [says he recites], "Blessed [art Thou, O Lord, our God, King of the Universe] who is true to his word to resurrect the dead."

Rabbi Hiyya in the name of Rabbi Yohanan [says he recites], "He who knows your numbers, He shall awaken you, He shall remove the dust from your eyes. Blessed [art Thou, O Lord, our God, King of the Universe,] who resurrects the dead."

Rabbi Eliezer in the name of Rabbi Hanina [says he recites], "He who created you with justice, and sustained you with justice, and removed you [from the world] with justice, and will resurrect you with justice; He who knows your numbers, He shall remove the dust from your eyes. Blessed [art Thou, O Lord, our God, King of the Universe,] who resurrects the dead."

— YERUSHALMI-TRACTATE BERAKHOT 9:1 III:8

The resurrection of the dead then marks the beginning of that process of restoration in response to Israelite repentance that God built into the very creation of the world. It also brings the final punishment to the gentiles, that is, those who do not know God. But, it goes without saying, through the Torah all humanity can know God in God's own self-revelation.

That explains why, since the Torah is a source of life, the angel of death holds off while sages study the Torah, but takes the sage — with a kiss — when he concludes his labor:

> Rabbi Seorim, brother of Raba, was sitting before Raba at his deathbed and saw him falling into a coma. Raba said to him, "Tell [the angel of death] not to torment me as I die."
>
> He said to him, "But aren't you his good buddy?"
>
> He said to him, "Since my star has been handed over into his control, he doesn't pay any attention to me any more."
>
> He said to him, "Show yourself to me in a dream." [Raba] did so.
>
> He asked him, "Did you suffer when you were dying?"
>
> He said to him, "No more than the prick of the leech."

> Raba was sitting before Rabbi Nahman at his deathbed and saw him falling into a coma. He said to him, "Tell [the angel of death] not to torment me as I die."
>
> He said to him, "But aren't you an eminent authority?"
>
> He said to him, "So who is eminent, who is regarded, who is treated as distinguished [by the angel of death]?"
>
> He said to him, "Show yourself to me in a dream." He did so.
>
> He asked him, "Did you suffer when you were dying?"
>
> He said to him, "No more than taking a piece of hair out of the milk, and, I have to tell you, if the Holy One, blessed be he, said to me, 'Now go back to that world as you were before,' I wouldn't do it, for the fear of death is too much to take."

> The angel of death made his appearance to Rabbi Sheshet in the market place. He said to him, "Are you going to take me in the market place like a dumb cow? Come to me at my home!"
>
> The angel of death made his appearance to Rabbi Ashi in the market place. He said to him, "Give me thirty days more so I can review my learning, since you say up there, 'Happy is he who comes up here bringing his learning all ready at hand.'"

So he came along thirty days later. He said to him, "So what's the rush?"

He said to him, "Rabbi Huna bar Nathan is on your heels, and 'no regime may impinge upon its fellow, even by so much as a hair's breadth.'"

The angel of death could not overcome Rabbi Hisda, because his mouth never ceased to recite his learning. He went out and sat on a cedar tree by the house of study. The branch of the cedar cracked, Rabbi Hisda stopped, and the other overcame him.

The angel of death could not get near Rabbi Hiyya. One day he appeared to him in the form of a poor beggar. He came and knocked on the door, saying, "Bring out some food for me." Others brought it out to him.

He said to Rabbi Hiyya, "Aren't you, my lord, going to treat with mercy this man who is standing outside?"

He opened the door to him, and he showed him a fiery rod and made him give up his soul.

— BABYLONIAN TALMUD TRACTATE MOED QATAN 28A

The intersection of the themes of Torah-study, the immortality of the soul, the humility of sages about all matters except for the Torah, and the sagacity of the sage all show us how, once more, the system says the same thing about everything.

Since sages identified Moses as "our rabbi" and maintained that, at Sinai, God had taught him the Torah, their account of how Moses died provides the best single picture of the good death:

At that time [the Holy One, blessed be He] said to the angel of death, "Go, bring me the soul of Moses."

The angel of death went and stood before him, saying to him, "Moses, give me your soul."

Moses grew angry with him and said to him, "Where I am sitting you have no right even to stand, yet you have said, 'Give me your soul'!" He threw him out with outrage.

Then the Holy One, blessed be He, said to Moses, "Moses, you have had enough of this world, for lo, the world to come is readied for you, for a place is prepared for you from the first six days of creation."

For it is said, "And the Lord said, Behold a place by me, and you shall stand upon the rock" (Exod. 33:21).

The Holy One, blessed be He, took the soul of Moses and stored it away under the throne of glory.

And when he took it, he took it only with a kiss, as it is said, "By the mouth of the Lord" (Deut. 34:5).

It is not the soul of Moses alone that is stored away under the throne of glory, but the souls of the righteous are stored away under the throne of glory, as it is said, "Yet the soul of my Lord shall be bound in the bundle of life with the Lord your God" (1 Sam. 25:29).

Is it possible to imagine that that is the case also with the souls of the wicked?

Scripture says, "And the souls of your enemies, those he shall sling out as from the hollow of a sling" (1 Sam. 25:29).

For even though one is tossed from place to place, it does not know on what to come to rest.

So, too, the souls of the wicked go roving and fluttering about the world and do not know where to come to rest.

The Holy One, blessed be He, further said to the angel of death, "Go, bring me the soul of Moses."

The angel of death went in search of him in his place but did not find him. He went to the Great Sea and said to it, "Has Moses come here?"

The sea replied, "From the day on which the Israelites passed through me, I have not seen him."

He went to the mountains and hills and said to them, "Has Moses come here?"

They replied, "From the day on which Israel received the Torah on Mount Sinai, we have not seen him.

He went to Sheol and Destruction and said to them, "Has Moses come here?"

They said to him, "His name we have heard, but him we have never seen."

He went to the ministering angels and said to them, "Has Moses come here?"

They said to him, "God understands his way and knows his place [cf. Job 28:23]. God has hidden him away for the life of the world to come, and no one knows where."

So it is said, "But wisdom, where shall it be found? And where is the place of understanding? Humanity does not know its price, nor is it found in the land of the living. The deep says, It is not in me, and the sea says, It is not with me.... Destruction and death say, We have heard a rumor thereof with our ears" (Job 28:13–15, 22).

Joshua too was seated and grieving for Moses, until the Holy One, blessed be He, said to him, "Joshua, why are you grieving for Moses? 'Moses, my servant, is dead' (Josh. 1:2)."

— THE FATHERS ACCORDING TO RABBI NATHAN XII:II.2–5

When a sage dies, the disciples grieve. But within the spirituality of Judaism, death is a homecoming.

FOUR

The Christian's Transformation at Death

Jesus, Paul, and the Promise of Resurrection

Jesus pictured life with God as involving such a radical change that ordinary human relationships would no longer prevail. Because that change, in all its comprehensiveness, was finally to the good, death — an intrinsic part of the way God changes our lives — was portrayed, deliberately and explicitly, as an opportunity, not a misfortune. To lose one's life, Jesus said, is to save it (see Matt. 16:23; Mark 8:35; Luke 9:24; John 12:25). That central assertion of Christianity is often treated as if it were poetic or paradoxical, but in fact it expresses a core element around which Jesus' teaching as a whole is constructed.

Jesus' profound confidence in God's will to change us radically brought with it a commitment to the language of eschatology, of the ultimate transformation which God both promised and threatened. Although Jesus' eschatology was sophisticated, there is no mistaking his emphasis on future transformation.[1] Some efforts have been made recently to discount the eschatological dimension of Jesus' teaching; they have not prevailed. Periodically, theologians in the West have attempted to convert Jesus' perspective into their own sense that the world is a static and changeless entity, but that appears to have been far from his own orientation.[2]

Although the eschatological character of Jesus' thinking is widely recognized, consensus is much more difficult to come by when it concerns Jesus' understanding of what is to occur *to particular human beings* within

---

1. See Chilton, *Pure Kingdom. Jesus' Vision of God: Studying the Historical Jesus 1* (Eerdmans: Grand Rapids, 1996).

2. See Chilton, *The Kingdom of God in the Teaching of Jesus* (London: SPCK and Philadelphia: Fortress, 1984). For discussion since that time, and particularly the contribution of Marcus Borg, see *Pure Kingdom*.

God's disclosure of his kingdom. Resurrection, as usually defined, promises actual life to individual persons within God's global transformation of all things. Because Jesus, on a straightforward reading of the Gospels, does not say much about resurrection as such, there has been a lively dispute over whether he had any distinctive (or even emphatic) teaching in that regard.

Still, when Jesus does address the issue, what he says is in fact unequivocal. Sadducees are portrayed as asking a mocking question of Jesus, designed to disprove the possibility of resurrection.[3] Because Moses commanded that, were a man to die childless, his brother should raise up a seed for him, suppose there were seven brothers, the first of whom was married. If they all died childless in sequence, whose wife would the woman be in the resurrection (see Matt. 22:23–28; Mark 12:18–23; Luke 20:27–33)?

Jesus' response, within a context which is set up with painstaking completeness, is categorical and direct (following the description of Mark's Gospel):

> And there came to him Zadokites, who say there is not resurrection, and they interrogated him, saying, "Teacher, Mosheh wrote us that if someone's brother dies and leaves a wife behind, but does not leave a child, that his brother should take the wife and arouse a seed for his brother. There were seven brothers, and the first took a wife, died and did not leave a seed. The second took her and died and did not leave a seed behind; and the third similarly. And the seven did not leave a seed. Last of all the woman also died. In the resurrection, of which of them will she be wife. For the seven had her as wife?" Stated Yeshua to them, "For this are you not deceived, knowing neither the Writings nor the miracle of God?! Because when the dead arise they neither marry nor give in marriage, but are like angels in the heavens. But concerning the dead — that they are raised — have you not read in the book of Mosheh in the passage about the thornbush? — how God spoke to him saying, I am Avraham's God and Yitzchak's God and Ya'aqov's

---

3. Acts 23:8 makes out that the Sadducees deny resurrection altogether, and that is also the judgment of Josephus. I have argued that, despite their unequivocal statements (or rather, precisely because they are so unequivocal), we should be cautious about what the Sadducees denied; see *The Temple of Jesus. His Sacrificial Program within a Cultural History of Sacrifice* (University Park: Pennsylvania State University Press, 1992) 82. The Sadducees' position is attributed to them only by unsympathetic observers, such as Josephus (*War* 2 §165–166) and various Christians (Mark 12:18–27; Matt. 22:23–33; Luke 20:27–38; Acts 23:6–8).

God? He is not God of the dead, but of the living. You are much
deceived!"

There are two arguments developed here, one from Scripture and one
based on a comparison between angels and those who are resurrected.
Of the two arguments, the one from Scripture is the more immediately
fitting, an appeal both to the nature of God and to the evaluation of
the patriarchs in early Judaism. If God identifies himself with Abraham, Isaac, and Jacob, it must be that in his sight, they live. And those
three patriarchs — carefully chosen in Jesus' reflection — are indeed living principles of Judaism itself; they are Israel as chosen in the case
of Abraham (see Genesis 15), as redeemed in the case of Isaac (see
Genesis 22), and as struggling to identity in the case of Jacob (see Genesis 32). That evocation of patriarchal identity is implied, rather than
demonstrated, but the assumption is that the hearer is able to make
such connections between the text of Scripture and the fulfillment of
that Scripture within present experience.[4] Yet that implicit logic of the
argument from Scripture only makes the second argument seem all the
bolder by comparison.

The direct comparison between people in the resurrection and angels
is consonant with the thought that the patriarchs must live in the sight
of God, since angels are normally associated with God's throne (so, for
example, in Dan. 7:9–14). So once the patriarchs are held to be alive
before God, the comparison with angels is feasible. But Jesus' statement
is not only a theoretical assertion of the majesty of God, a majesty which
includes the patriarchs (and, by extension, the patriarchs' comparabil-
ity to the angels); it is also an emphatic claim of what we might call
divine anthropology. Jesus asserts that human relations, the usual basis
of human society and divisions among people (namely sexual identity),
are radically altered in the resurrection.[5] That claim of substantial re-

---

4. For Jesus' characteristic attitude towards Scripture, see Chilton, *A Galilean Rabbi and His
Bible. Jesus' Use of the Interpreted Scripture of His Time* (Wilmington: Glazier, 1984), also published
with the subtitle, *Jesus' Own Interpretation of Isaiah* (London: SPCK, 1984).

5. It is commonly asserted that Jesus accorded with accepted understandings of resurrection
within Judaism; see Pheme Perkins, *Resurrection. New Testament Witness and Contemporary Reflection* (London: Chapman, 1984) 75. That is an unobjectionable finding, but it leads to an odd
conclusion: "Nor can one presume that Jesus makes any significant contribution to or elaboration
of these common modes of speaking." Perkins is not clear about what she means here, or the basis
of her assertion. Does warning the reader against presuming that Jesus had something original to
say imply that he in fact said nothing original? Why speak of presumption at all, when there is
an actual saying to hand? But the analysis of the saying is also confused, because Perkins speaks
of it as invented by Mark when it has anything new to say, and as routine insofar as it may be
attributed to Jesus. The discussion typifies the ill-defined program of trivializing the place of Jesus

generation and transcendence became a major theme among the more theological thinkers who followed Jesus, beginning with Paul.

But before we turn to Paul, the first great interpreter of Jesus, we need to address a preliminary question: how is it that Jesus' position in regard to the resurrection is only spelled out in one passage within the Gospels? There is a general explanation which might be offered in this regard, but it is only partially satisfactory. The intents of the Synoptic Gospels, on the one hand, and of the Fourth Gospel, on the other hand, are quite different. The Synoptics are designed in the interests of catechesis, for the preparation of proselytes for baptism, while the Gospel according to John is homiletic. What was in all probability the original ending of John states the purpose as maintaining the faith of believers so that they might go on to have life in the name of Christ (John 20:31), while the introduction to Luke speaks of the things which the reader has only recently learned (Luke 1:1–4, and the verb is *katêkheo*).[6] In between the initial preparation of catechumens and the advanced interpretation offered to those well beyond that point, a great deal of instruction naturally took place.

The Lord's Prayer provides a stunning example of the kind of teaching that may have fallen in between initial catechesis and homiletics in some communities. John's Gospel contains no version of the Prayer, presumably because it is assumed as elementary knowledge. But then, Mark's Gospel also omits it, but for a different reason: the assumption is that oral instruction, apart from public catechesis, is to *complement* what the catechumen learns from the Gospel. The Prayer is by no means advanced knowledge; after all, the catechumen will have to learn to say *Abbá* at baptism (see Gal. 4:6; Rom. 8:15) and to know what that means. Yet were our knowledge of Jesus and early Christianity limited to Mark and John among the Gospels, we would not be aware of the Prayer or of its importance within the teaching of Jesus and the practice of his movement.

Teaching in regard to the resurrection may be held to belong more to an intermediate level of instruction within early Christianity than to a preparatory or advanced level. After all, Mark's Gospel relates no story of the appearance of the risen Jesus, but only the narrative of the empty tomb (Mark 16:1–8). The silence of the women at the tomb is the last

---

within the tradition of the New Testament by critics who once tended to exaggerate the literary aspirations of those who composed the documents.

6. For further discussion of the relationship between John and the Synoptics in terms of their social functions, see Chilton, *Profiles of a Rabbi. Synoptic Opportunities in Reading about Jesus: Brown Judaic Studies 177* (Atlanta: Scholars Press, 1989).

word in the Gospel, and it is an approving word. The Markan community is thereby instructed to maintain reserve in the face of persecution. But it is very clear what that reserve is about: the young man at the tomb (Mark 16:6–7) and Jesus himself at an earlier stage (Mark 8:31; 9:9, 31; 10:33–34) leave no doubt that the full disclosure of Jesus' identity lies in his resurrection. As the Markan catechumen approaches the Paschal Mystery, when baptism will occur and full access to eucharist extended for the first time, the door to the truth of Jesus' resurrection is opened in the Gospel, but actual entry to that truth awaits further (perhaps private) instruction.[7]

But the analogy between the handling of the resurrection of Jesus in the Gospels and the handling of the Lord's Prayer is only partial. First, the apparent lack of Mark is made up by Matthew (6:9–13) and Luke (11:2–4), and together those Gospels provide a cogent representation of the model of prayer which Jesus taught, a model which is not without echo in the Gospels according to Mark and John.[8] Second, the resurrection of Jesus is actually introduced as a topic in Mark, only then to be omitted at the end of the Gospel. When that lacuna is made up in Matthew, Luke, and John (as well as in the artificial ending provided Mark itself in many manuscripts), the result is a series of stories whose cogency does not approach that of the Lord's Prayer in Matthew and Luke.

So it will not do to try to invoke a general explanation, in terms of the level of instruction involved, to account for the absence or the discordance of stories of Jesus' resurrection and for the relative paucity of Jesus' own teaching regarding resurrection within the Gospels. Rather, there seems to have been a deliberate policy of esotericism in this regard. To some extent, the silence of the women in Mark is an index of this policy, and the possibility of persecution for belief in the name of Jesus which their silence doubtless reflects offers (once again) a partial explanation for the counsel of silence. But all of these explanations which involve the happenstance of history — the educational pitch of the Gospels, the esoteric practice of early Christianity, the pressures exerted by the pos-

---

7. To this extent, the so-called "Secret Gospel of Mark" which Morton Smith identified and popularized may provide an insight into the post-catechetical moment in early Christianity. But of course, the controversy concerning that work does not permit any conclusions to be drawn on the basis of Smith's contribution alone. See James H. Charlesworth and Craig A. Evans, "Jesus in the Agrapha and Apocryphal Gospels," *Studying the Historical Jesus. Evaluations of the State of Current Research: New Testament Tools and Studies XIX* (ed. B. Chilton and C. A. Evans; Leiden: Brill, 1994) 479–533, 526–532.

8. See Chilton, *Jesus' Prayer and Jesus' Eucharist: His Personal Practice of Spirituality* (Valley Forge: Trinity Press International, 1997).

sibility of persecution for belief in Jesus' resurrection — do not account for the qualitative difference in the manner of handling the resurrection as compared, say, to the Lord's Prayer. And after all: the resurrection of Jesus is on any known reading the most obviously distinctive element in Christian teaching: how can there be a lack of cogency in providing for instruction on this point within the Gospels?

Together with those explanations, which may be characterized in terms of their reference to extrinsic circumstances, we must consider the intrinsic structure of belief in Jesus' resurrection as received and practiced within early Christianity. Something about the way belief in the resurrection was structured, within the social and historical environment which has already been described, produced the apparent lacuna and the evident discrepancies we have referred to within the textual tradition and what produced that tradition. Mark is a good initial guide to the complexity of that structure. The young man at the tomb tells the women to tell the disciples and Peter that Jesus goes before them into Galilee, and that they will see Jesus there (Mark 16:7). That is, Peter is identified as the central named witness of Jesus' resurrection, but then no actual appearance to Peter is conveyed. Instead, the Gospel ends.

"The Lord has risen, and has appeared to Simon" (Luke 24:34) is the acclamation — widely recognized as primitive (compare 1 Cor. 15:5) — which Luke alone relates, but here again, no actual story is attached to this statement. Instead, Luke then gives us, in addition to a recognizable but distinctive narrative of the empty tomb (Luke 24:1–12), the story of Jesus' appearance to the two disciples who were on their way to Emmaus (Luke 24:13–35). That story emphasizes that Jesus was not instantly recognizable to the disciples, and he disappears once they finally do recognize him in Emmaus itself; the theme is explicitly given as Jesus' manifestation in the breaking of bread (v. 35), which occurs in the evidently liturgical context of the reminiscence of Jesus and the interpretation of Scripture (vv. 18–27). So alongside the narrative of the empty tomb, which anticipates that Jesus' resurrection involves the physical body which was buried, there is a story which portrays the resurrection in straightforwardly visionary and eucharistic terms: Jesus is seen, but not recognized, then recognized, and no longer seen. The conflict with the story of the empty tomb is manifest, and all the more so as it is actually referred to by Kleopas in what he says to the stranger who turns out to be the risen Jesus (vv. 22–23).

Luke's Gospel is designed to resolve that conflict to some extent. That design is reflected in the way the Gospel smooths out the problem which would have been caused by telling the disciples to go to Galilee (as in Mark), since the risen Jesus appears only in the vicinity of Jerusalem in Luke. Instead, Luke's two men (rather than one young man) remind the women of what Jesus said *when he was in Galilee* (Luke 24:4–8). That enables the focus to remain Jerusalem, where the appearance to Simon occurred, and in whose vicinity the disclosure of the risen Jesus was experienced in the breaking of bread. In that same Jerusalem (never Galilee in Luke), Jesus appears in the midst of the disciples in the context of another meal (also associated with the interpretation of Scripture and the recollection of Jesus), and shows them that he is flesh and bone, not spirit. He commissions them, instructing them to remain in Jerusalem until the power to become witnesses comes upon them. Leading them out to Bethany, he is taken up to heaven while he is in the act of blessing them (Luke 24:36–52). This final appearance in Luke fulfills the expectations raised by the empty tomb and is a triumph of harmonization: Jesus not only says he is flesh and bone, he shows his hands and his feet, offers to be touched, asks for food and eats it (vv. 38–43). Yet this physical emphasis is also synthesized with the visionary and liturgical idiom of what happened near and at Emmaus. But in all of this, interestingly, there is silence regarding Peter's experience.

Matthew returns the focus to Galilee, *and to Galilee alone*, as the locus of the risen Jesus. Here Jesus himself actually encounters the women as they run to tell the disciples what the angel has said, and he tells them to instruct his brothers to go to Galilee (Matt. 28:10). The reference to "brothers" at this point, rather than to "disciples" (cf. 28:7), is apparently deliberate; the angel speaks to the women disciples, while Jesus is adding an injunction for a distinct group. After the story about the guard and the High Priests (Matt. 28:11–15), however, the last passage in the Gospel according to Matthew, the appearance of Jesus in Galilee, concerns only the eleven disciples. They see and worship (and doubt), receiving the commission to baptize all nations in the knowledge that Jesus is always with them. In its own way, and centered in Galilee rather than in Jerusalem, Matthew achieves what Luke achieves: the appearances of the risen Jesus are visionary (and almost abstract), but the explanation of that vision is that his body was raised. The experience of the earthquake and the angel by the guards and their willingness to broadcast the lie (concocted by high priests and elders) that Jesus' body had been stolen (Matt. 28:2–4, 11–15) underscores that explanation. What remains startling about Matthew is the complete absence of direct reference to Peter in this context (compare Matt. 28:7 to Mark 16:7), although Peter is singled out for special treatment in the same Gospel (see Matt. 16:17–19).

Matthew's silence regarding Peter and Luke's laconic reference to the tradition that he was the first to have the Lord appear to him call attention to the structural oddity in testimony to Jesus' resurrection in the New Testament. Simon Kephas/Peter is held to be the fountainhead of this faith (as in 1 Cor. 15:5), but the Synoptic Gospels simply do not convey a tradition of the appearance to Peter in particular. John's Gospel puts Peter and the other disciple whom Jesus loved at the site of the empty tomb.[9] The other disciple is said to have seen the tomb and to have believed, but Peter only sees (John 20:1–10). Mary Magdalene then sees two angels and Jesus, but does not recognize him at first and is forbidden to touch him: her commission is to tell the brothers that he goes to the Father (John 20:11–18). Likewise, Jesus' commission at this point is simply to go to the Father, which presupposes — as Benoit points out — that in what follows any descent from the Father is only for the purpose of appearing to the disciples.[10]

Commissioning is the purpose of Jesus in what follows. He appears among the disciples when the doors were shut for fear of the Jews, and provides Holy Spirit for forgiving and confirming sins (John 20:19–23).[11] During the appearance, he shows his hands and his side in order to be recognized (20:20), which he does again in a second appearance, this time for the benefit of Thomas, and with the offer to feel his hands and his side (John 20:24–29). Obviously, the coalescing of the empty tomb

---

9. Luke 24:12 puts Peter alone there. For a defense of that tradition as historical, see Pierre Benoit, *Passion et résurrection du Seigneur* (Paris: Cerf, 1985) 288–290. But Benoit's attempt to make John's Gospel the nearest point to the fountainhead of such traditions is not convincing. John rather seems to aggregate the elements already present within the Synoptic Gospels. Mark's young man becomes the other disciple, Luke's reference to Peter's presence at the tomb is expanded, Matthew's description of Jesus' manifestation to the women is turned into a private appearance to Mary Magdalene, Luke's tradition of appearances to the disciples in Jerusalem during meals is honored with a cognate emphasis on both visionary and physical aspects, and Matthew's localization (together with Mark's promise) of such an event, also with much less physical emphasis and in Galilee, is also respected.

10. Benoit, p. 291. He goes on to suggest that the return of Jesus after this point must be "totally spiritualized, in particular in the Eucharist." That suggests the extent to which the Gospel has shifted idioms within its presentation of the resurrection. He deals with the story of what happened near Emmaus in much the same way, pp. 297–325.

11. An evident echo of Matt. 16:17–19, the placement of which here serves to highlight Peter's importance within the tradition of the resurrection, without actually solving the problem that, by the implication of John 20:6–9, Peter saw the empty tomb, but did not believe as the other disciple did. John 21 will return to the question of Peter, reflecting an awareness that his place within what has been said has not yet been resolved.

and the visionary appearances has continued in John, but the problem of Simon Peter has not so far been resolved.

That resolution comes in the close of the present text of John, which is widely considered an addendum or appendix (John 21).[12] Here, Peter and six other disciples are fishing on the sea of Galilee, and Jesus appears on the shore unrecognized, asking if they have anything to eat. They have not caught anything all night, but at Jesus' command they cast their net and catch more fish than they can pull up. The disciples whom Jesus loves recognizes Jesus and informs Peter who the stranger is. Peter leaps into the water, and swims to shore, followed by the others in the boat. Jesus, whose identity none dares to ask, directs the preparation of breakfast from the 153 large fish which were caught. Finally, Peter himself is commissioned to shepherd the flock of Jesus.

Although this third appearance of the risen Jesus in John is the only appearance which features Peter,[13] the allusions to baptism and the direction of the Church make it clear that it is far from the sort of tradition which would have been formed in any immediate proximity to Peter's experience. Still, one feature stands out. As in the story of what happened near and at Emmaus (which holds the place of an appearance to Peter in Luke), Jesus is not immediately known; his identity is a matter of inference (see John 21:7, 12 and Luke 24:16, 31). This, of course, is just the direction in which all of the Gospels are *not* headed by their structuring of traditions. They anticipate an instantly recognizable Jesus, fully continuous with the man who was buried: that is the point of the story of the empty tomb in all four Gospels.

Their insistence on the physical continuity of the buried and risen Jesus is reflected in the way they present other stories. Jesus raises to life the son of the widow of Nain (Luke 7:11–17), the daughter of Jairus (Matt. 9:18–19, 23–26; Mark 5:21–24, 35–43; Luke 8:40–42, 49–56), and Lazarus (John 11:1–46). An excellent study has shown that all of these stories represent the conviction that Jesus' resurrection promised the resurrection of the faithful.[14] But that connection also worked the other way: expectations of how the resurrection was to happen generally influenced the presentation of how the risen Jesus appeared. When

---

12. See Benoit, 327–353.

13. It has been argued that the Gospel of Peter represents a more primitive tradition, but the fact is that the text incorporates elements from the canonical Gospels. It appears to be a pastiche, much in the vein of the longer ending of Mark. See Charlesworth and Evans, pp. 503–514.

14. See Gérard Rochais, *Les récits de résurrection des morts dans le Nouveau Testament: Society for New Testament Studies Monograph Series 40* (Cambridge: Cambridge University Press, 1981).

Paul insisted that "flesh and blood cannot inherit the kingdom of God" (1 Cor. 15:50), he was not opposing an abstract proposition.[15] Indeed, it would seem on the face of the matter to contradict the statement in 1 Thess. 4:13–18 that the dead will be raised and presented with the living, snatched up into the air for that purpose, so as always to be with the Lord. That literally physical belief in the general resurrection, which has been styled "apocalyptic,"[16] influenced the portrayal of Jesus' resurrection, and is most manifest in the story of the empty tomb.

Within his discussion of 1 Cor. 15:50 in its wider context, Peter Carnley concludes with a telling insight:

> It is clear that Paul is struggling imaginatively to explain the nature of the resurrection body. This suggests that, whatever his Damascus road experience was, it was sufficiently ambiguous and unclear as not to be of real help in explaining the detailed nature of the body of the resurrection. The evidence thus leads us back to the view that his initial experiential encounter with the raised Christ was in the nature of some kind of "heavenly vision." The fact that the nature of the body of the resurrection seems to have been open to speculation indicates that this was indeed a speculative matter that was brought up rather than settled by the encounter with the raised Jesus on the Damascus road.[17]

Carnley goes on the analyze the appearance of Jesus in Matthew in similar terms, and he points out that Acts 26:19 formally describes Paul encounter with the risen Jesus as a "heavenly vision."[18] Carnley does not observe that Paul himself claimed he had "seen our Lord Jesus" (1 Cor. 9:1) and included himself in the record of those to whom Jesus "appeared" (1 Cor. 15:8, cf. v. 5). But those citations only strengthen Carnley's overall point, that vision is the fundamental category within which the initial experience of Jesus as risen was apprehended (p. 245).[19]

---

15. In this case, Paul is stating something with which his readers would have agreed. The disagreement with some in Corinth is not over whether there is to be a resurrection, but what resurrection is to involve. See A. J. M. Wedderburn, *Baptism and Resurrection. Studies in Pauline Theology against Its Graeco-Roman Background: Wissenschaftliche Untersuchungen zum Neuen Testament 44* (Tübingen: Mohr, 1987) 35–36. Given Paul's form of words in 1 Cor. 15:29, the tendency to make any disagreement about resurrection into a denial is evident (cf. n. 3 above).

16. Rochais, 187. See also Kenneth Grayston, *Dying, We Live. A New Enquiry into the Death of Christ in the New Testament* (New York: Oxford University Press, 1990) 13.

17. Peter Carnley, *The Structure of Resurrection Belief* (Oxford: Clarendon, 1987) 233.

18. Carnley, pp. 237–238.

19. Similarly, see Francis Schüssler Fiorenza, *Foundational Theology. Jesus and the Church* (New York: Crossroads, 1984) 35–37.

The narrative of the empty tomb, a relatively late tradition within the Gospels (as the consensus of scholarship would have it), functions to explain the theophany of the risen Jesus, although in itself it is not a theophany.[20] That is why John 20:6–9 can put Simon Peter on the site of the empty tomb, and yet not attribute belief in the resurrection of Jesus to him.

Care should be taken, however, not to assimilate the language of literal vision to the description in Acts of what Paul did or did not see on the road to Damascus. In chapter 9, those around Paul hear the voice, but see nothing (Acts 9:7): the light blinds Paul, which is what brings him to Ananias and baptism (Acts 9:3–18). In chapter 22, Paul is quoted as saying his companions saw the light, but did not hear the voice (22:9), and that may be consistent with the sense of what he says later (Acts 26:12–18). A hasty reference to the materials of vision in Acts has led to the suggestion that the resurrection is associated with an experience of a heavenly light (*Lichtglanz*).[21] The portrayal of Paul's vision of the risen Jesus in Acts surely warns us away from reducing the experience to a single sensation and rather emphasizes the importance of being in the presence of one identified as Jesus who commissions the recipient of the vision to a divine purpose. The "vision" or "appearance," so designated because the verbal usage "he appeared" (*ôphthê*) is preferred in the New Testament, involves the awareness — mediated by a variety of senses and apprehensions — that Jesus is indeed present to one, and present so as to convey a divine imperative.

Those twin emphases, the identity of Jesus and the commissioning, underlie all stories of the actual appearance of the risen Jesus (and are not present in the later narrative of the empty tomb). In his recent study, Francis Schüssler Fiorenza has shown that the appearances of Jesus in the New Testament serve neither to console people generally about immortality nor to make an abstract point about God's eschatological victory.[22] Rather, "in almost all the stories the identity motif is present because even in appearances to the group he is either not recognized or recognized only with doubt and suspicion, so that he must confirm his identify before commissioning them."[23]

---

20. That statement is only accurate, of course, if the qualifying statement ("in itself") is observed. As soon as the young man or men are taken as angels, and more especially when the risen Jesus himself appears on the scene, the story of the empty tomb becomes theophanic. But the bulk of scholarship, and simple common sense, evaluate those elements as embellishments.

21. For a suitably cautious assessment, see Carnley, 240–242.

22. *Foundational Theology*, 45.

23. *Foundational Theology*, 37.

That insight, which conforms with the analysis here, comports with Paul's capacity to claim that he has seen the Lord (1 Cor. 9:1) and at the same time to refer to that moment as when it pleased God to reveal his Son in him (Gal. 1:15–16). The conviction of divine presence, identified with Jesus and inciting to a commission, defines the content of the experience that he had been raised from the dead. That definition does justice to the narratives of Jesus' appearance in the Gospels, to Paul's experience, and to the appearance to James as given in the Gospel of the Hebrews.[24] In the last case, James is informed by Jesus that he, as son of man, has risen from the dead. In that case as well as in the others, the language of effective personal presence more accurately conveys the scene than does the language of vision. "Vision," we might conclude, is the overall category of experience in which our sources would place the resurrection of Jesus, but the experience was of his effectively divine and personal presence after his death.

Jesus' own teaching involved a refusal to grant an assumption of physical resurrection, the continuity of marital relationships, and in so doing he disappointed the expectations raised by the story of the empty tomb, as well as the stories of the raisings of the son of the widow of Nain, of Jairus' daughter, and of Lazarus. The increasingly physical terms of reference of early Christian teaching, as in 1 Thess. 4:13–18, complicated the structure of the traditions of Jesus' resurrection and of his teaching concerning the resurrection. There is little of Jesus' teaching preserved for the same reason that there is only an echo of Peter's experience of the risen Jesus: in both cases, the challenge to the assumptions of the story of the empty tomb was too great to be incorporated into the tradition of the Gospels.

Jesus' teaching of a radical alteration at the point of death underscores that Christianity's hope is not of a survival or a reincarnation of some remnant of our personalities. Rather, death is understood to be a watershed, such that the current configuration of relationships and of reality is wiped away. Part of the transformation of this world into the kingdom is that, as Paul put, "the form of this world is passing away" (1 Cor. 7:31). That is not in any sense a fatalistic statement. Rather, Paul is appropriating Jesus' hopeful teaching about the eschatological transformation of all things. From that perspective, the death of the individual, and the

---

24. Cited in Jerome's *Famous Men* 2; see Edgar Hennecke and Wilhelm Schneemelcher (tr. R. McL. Wilson), *New Testament Apocrypha* (London: SCM, 1973).

removal of the present form of the world, point towards the new thing God is about to do with all of us.

It is for this reason that Christianity in principle does not differentiate between the types of death which come to people. To take to oneself the right to decide when death occurs, whether another's or one's own, cannot be encouraged, because that is an attempt to legislate when God will act in relation to a human being. But except for that arrogance, all forms of death are opportunities for resurrection, even death on a cross.

The why and the how of death within the perspective of Christianity involve a fundamental reversal of what most people expect to find. Instead of a punishment, death is an opportunity; instead of a careful training for a peaceful departure as an ideal, the stark fact of a basic interruption of life is emphasized. That fundamental reversal, however, is in the service of the expectation of what occurs after death. A statement of Paul's in his letter to the Philippians is classic (Phil. 1:21–24):

> Because to me to live is Christ, and to die is gain. Yet if to live in flesh is the harvest of my work, I do not know what I shall choose. But I am constrained between the two, having a desire to leave and to be with Christ, very much better, but to remain in flesh, the more necessary for you.

Philippians was probably written after Paul's death, but on the basis of the memory of what his companions remembered of his own mature positions and attitudes. In the present case, there is an exceptional clarity in regard to the actual focus of ethical striving within Christianity. The measure of that struggle is the spiritual inheritance which awaits the follower of Jesus, rather than compensation in terms of this world. That is because the actual purpose of being alive is to achieve spirit, and on that basis to know a life which is no longer limited to the flesh and the self. Death is the closure of that limited existence, and therefore holds out the prospect of a complete transformation into the realm of spirit.

Within the Christian emphasis upon spiritual transformation, the sense of Christianity's teaching in regard to sin becomes plain. Paul wrote in his letter to the Romans (7:14–25):

> For we know that the law is spiritual; but I am of flesh, sold under sin. Because what I achieve I do not know: for what I do not want, this I accomplish, but what I hate is what I do. But if what I do not want is what I do, I agree that law is worthwhile. And now it is no longer I who achieve it, but sin dwelling in me. For I know

that nothing good dwells in me, that is in my flesh, because to want lies within me, but to achieve the worthwhile does not. Because I do not do the good I want, but the evil which I do not want, this I accomplish. But if what I do not want is what I do, I am no longer achieving it, but the sin dwelling in me. Therefore I find this law: when I wish to do the worthwhile, the bad lies within me. Because I recognize the law of God by the inner person, but I see another law in my members, warring against the law of my mind and taking me prisoner by the law of sin which is in my members. I am a miserable person! Who will save me from the body of this death? Thanks to God through Christ Jesus our Lord. So therefore: I serve God's law with the mind, but with flesh sin's law.

The fact of human limitation is there all our lives, written in our failed projects of improvement. Paul understands this condition not as the circumstance of individual, tortured psychology, but as inherently human. In the very act of aspiring to what is good, people provoke a resistance in their midst which assures their failure.

Finally, this teaching became known as that of original (in the sense of inherent) sin. Christianity is frequently charged with being too pessimistic in its assessment of people for that reason. A case can be made for the view that human history better accords with a teaching of inherent human sin than it does with faith in human progress. In fact, Augustine made out just that argument (among others) in his classic work, *The City of God*. In the end, however, the Christian doctrine of original sin is not grounded in the observation of human behavior. Its ground is rather the eschatological hope of the transformation which is to come. The promise of grace, sealed by the Spirit of God and anticipating a glorious fulfillment, makes it apparent by contrast that, just as the form of this world is passing away, so our human complicity in the failures of this world is also to be transcended.

Paul's classic discussion of the issue of the resurrection in 1 Corinthians 15 clearly represents his continuing commitment to the categorical understanding of the resurrection which Jesus initiated. The particular occasion of his teaching is the apparent denial of the resurrection on the part of some people in Corinth (1 Cor. 15:12b): "How can some of you say that there is no resurrection of the dead?"[25] His address of that denial

---

25. For a survey of attempts to explain this statement, see A. J. M. Wedderburn, *Baptism and Resurrection. Studies in Pauline Theology against Its Graeco-Roman Background: Wissenschaftliche Untersuchungen zum Neuen Testament 44* (Tübingen: Mohr, 1987) pp. 6–37. He comes to no

is first of all on the basis of the integrity of apostolic preaching. Indeed, Paul prefaces his question with the earliest extant catalog of the traditions regarding Jesus' resurrection (1 Cor. 15:1–11). That record makes it plain why so much variety within stories of the appearance of the risen Jesus in the Gospels was possible: reference is made to a separate appearance to Cephas, then to the Twelve, then to more than five hundred "brothers" (cf. Matt. 28:10!), then to James, then to "all the apostles," and then finally to Paul himself (vv. 5–8). The depth and range of that catalog is what enables Paul to press on to his first argument against the Corinthian denial of the resurrection (15:13–14): "But if there is no resurrection of the dead, neither has Christ been raised; and if Christ has not been raised, then our preaching is empty and your faith is empty!"

Paul expands on this argument in what follows (1 Cor. 15:15–19), but the gist of what he says in that section is as simple as what he says at first: faith in Jesus' resurrection logically requires our affirmation of the reality of resurrection generally. That may seem to be an argument entirely from hypothesis, until we remember that Paul sees the moment when belief in Jesus occurs as the occasion of our reception of the Spirit of God (so Gal. 4:4–6):

> When the fullness of time came, God sent forth his Son, born from woman, born under law, so that he might redeem those under law, in order that we might obtain Sonship. And because you are sons, God sent the Spirit of his Son into your hearts, crying, "Abba! Father!"

Because the Spirit in baptism is nothing other than the living Spirit of God's Son, Jesus' resurrection is attested by the very fact of the primordially Christian experience of faith. The availability of his Spirit shows that he has been raised from the dead. In addition, the preaching in his name formally claims his resurrection, so that to deny resurrection as a whole is to make the apostolic preaching into a lie: empty preaching, as Paul says, and therefore empty faith.

Paul's emphasis in this context on the spiritual integrity of the apostolic preaching, attested in baptismal experience, is coherent with Jesus' earlier claim that the Scriptures warrant the resurrection (since God is God of the living, rather than of the dead). Implicitly, Paul accords the apostolic preaching the same sort of authority which Jesus attributed to

---

finding regarding what view Paul meant to attribute to some Corinthians, but he seems correct in affirming that a simple denial on their part (despite the form of words Paul uses) is unlikely. More likely, Paul was dealing with people who did not agree with his teaching of a bodily resurrection.

the Scriptures of Israel. Paul also proceeds — in a manner comparable to Jesus' argument — to an argument on the basis of the category of humanity which the resurrection involves: he portrays Jesus as the first of those raised from the dead. Where Jesus himself had compared those to be resurrected to angels, Paul compares them to Jesus. His resurrection is what provides hope for the resurrection of the dead as a whole (1 Cor. 15:20–28).

That hope, Paul goes on to argue, is what permits the Corinthians themselves to engage in the practice of being baptized on behalf of the dead (15:29).[26] The practice assumes that, when the dead come to be raised, even if they have not been baptized during life, baptism on their behalf after their death will confer benefit. Similarly, Paul takes his own courage as an example of the hopeful attitude which must assume the resurrection of the dead as its ground: why else would Christians encounter the dangers that they do (15:30–32a)?

The claim of resurrection, then, does not only involve a hope based upon a reception of Spirit and the promise of Scripture (whether in the form of the Scriptures of Israel or the apostolic preaching). Resurrection as an actual hope impinges directly upon what we conceive becomes of persons as we presently know them after they have died. (And that, of course, will immediately influence our conception of people as they are now perceived and how we might engage with them.) Paul's argument therefore cannot and does not rest solely on assertions of the spiritual integrity of the biblical witness and the apostolic preaching. He must also spell out an anthropology of resurrection, such that the spiritual hope and the Scriptural witness are worked out within the terms of reference of human experience.

Precisely when he does that in 1 Corinthians 15, Paul develops a Christian metaphysics. He does so by comparing people in the resurrection, not to angels, as Jesus himself had done, but — as we have seen — to the resurrected Jesus. And that comparison functions for Paul both because Jesus is preached as raised from the dead and because, within the experience of baptism, Jesus is known as the living source of the Spirit of God.[27] Jesus as raised from the dead is the point of departure for Paul's thinking about the resurrection, and because his focus is a

---

26. For a discussion of the practice in relation to Judaic custom (cf. 2 Macc. 12:40–45), see Ethelbert Stauffer (tr. J. Marsh), *New Testament Theology* (New York: Macmillan, 1955) 299 n. 544. C. K. Barrett also comes to the conclusion that the vicarious effect of baptism is at issue, *A Commentary on the First Epistle to the Corinthians* (London: Black, 1968) 362–364, although he is somewhat skeptical of Stauffer's analysis.

27. As Perkins (p. 227) puts it, "These associations make it clear that the resurrection of Jesus

particular human being, his analysis of the resurrection is much more systematic than Jesus'.

When Paul thinks of a person, he conceives of a body as composed of flesh. Flesh in his definition is physical substance, which varies from one created thing to another (for example, people, animals, birds, and fish [1 Cor. 15:35–39]). But in addition to being physical bodies, people are also what Paul calls a "psychic body," by which he means bodies with souls (1 Cor. 15:44). (Unfortunately, the phrase is wrongly translated in many modern versions, but its dependence on the noun for "soul" [*psukhê*] shows what the real sense is.)[28] In other words, people as bodies are not just lumps of flesh, but they are self-aware. That self-awareness is precisely what makes them "psychic body."

Now in addition to being physical body and psychic body, Paul says we are (or can become) "spiritual body" (1 Cor. 15:44). That is, we can relate thoughts and feelings to one another and to God, as 1 Cor. 2:9–16 shows us. Jesus is therefore the last Adam, a "life-giving Spirit" (1 Cor. 15:45) just as the first Adam was a "living being" or "soul" (the two words are the same in Greek, *psukhê*). Jesus is the basis on which we can realize our identities as God's children, the brothers and sisters of Christ, and know the power of the resurrection.

The metaphysics of both Christology and spirituality are the same: they relate Christ to creation and believers to God, because in each the principle is the eschatological transformation of human nature by means of Spirit. "Flesh" and "soul" become, not ends in themselves, but way stations on the course to "Spirit."

Just as sin marks out the necessity of human transformation in the realm of ethics, so physical death marks out the necessity of human transformation in the realm of its medium of existence. When Paul describes that existential transformation, his thinking becomes openly and irreducibly metaphysical (1 Cor. 15:35–44):

> But someone will say, How are the dead raised, and with what
> sort of body do they come? Fool, what you yourself sow does not
> become alive unless it dies! And what do you sow? You sow not
> the body which shall be, but a bare seed, perhaps of wheat or of

had been understood from an early time as the eschatological turning point of the ages and not merely as the reward for Jesus as a righteous individual."

28. The adjective does not mean "physical" as we use that word. Although that is a simple point, it apparently requires some emphasis. Scholars of Paul routinely assert that Paul is speaking of some sort of physical resurrection, when that is exactly what Paul denies. See Tom Wright, *What Did Paul Really Say?* (Grand Rapids: Eerdmans, 1997) 50.

another grain. But God gives to it a body just as he wills, and to each of the germs its own body. Not all flesh is the same flesh, but there is one of human beings, another flesh of animals, another flesh of birds, another of fish. And there are heavenly bodies and earthly bodies, but one is the glory of the heavenly and another of the earthly. One glory is the sun's and another the moon's, and another glory of stars, because star differs from star in glory. So also is the resurrection of the dead. Sown in corruption, it is raised in incorruption; sown in dishonor, it is raised in glory; sown in weakness, it is raised in power; sown a physical body, it is raised a spiritual body.

There is not a more exact statement of the process of resurrection in the whole of Christian literature, and Paul's words have had a firm place in Christian liturgies of burial. Their particular genius is the insight that resurrection involves a new creative act by God, what Paul elsewhere calls a "new creation" (2 Cor. 5:17; Gal. 6:15). But God's new creation is not simply an event which commences at death. Rather, a progressive transformation joins the realm of ethics together with the realm of metaphysics. Morally and existentially, the hope of the resurrection involves a fresh, fulfilled humanity.

Origen and the Dialectics of Resurrection

Born in 185 c.e. in Egypt, Origen knew the consequences which faith could have in the Roman world: his father died in the persecution of Severus in 202. Origen accepted the sort of renunciation demanded of apostles in the Gospels, putting aside his possessions to develop what Eusebius calls the philosophical life demanded by Jesus (see Eusebius, *History of the Church,* 6.3). His learning resulted in his appointment to the catechetical school in Alexandria, following the great examples of Pantaenus and Clement. Origen later moved to Caesarea in Palestine, as a result of a bitter dispute with Demetrius, the Bishop of Alexandria. Indeed, Origen remained a controversial figure after his death (and until this day), to a large extent because he wrestled more profoundly than most thinkers with the consequences of Spirit's claim on the flesh. In his treatment of the resurrection, Origen shows himself a brilliant exegete and a profound theologian. He sees clearly that, in 1 Corinthians 15, Paul insists that the resurrection from the dead must be bodily. And

Origen provides the logical grounding of Paul's claim (see Origen, *On First Principles,* 2.10.1):

> If it is certain that we are to be possessed of bodies, and if those bodies that have fallen are declared to rise again — and the expression "rise again" could not properly be used except of that which had previously fallen — then there can be no doubt that these bodies rise again in order that at the resurrection we may once more be clothed with them.

But Origen equally insists upon Paul's assertion that "flesh and blood cannot inherit the kingdom of God" (1 Cor. 15:50). There must be a radical transition from flesh to spirit, as God fashions a body which can dwell in the heavens (*On First Principles,* 2.10.3).

Origen pursues the point of this transition into a debate with fellow Christians (*On First Principles,* 2.10.3):

> We now direct the discussion to some of our own people, who either from want of intellect or from lack of instruction introduce an exceedingly low and mean idea of the resurrection of the body. We ask these people in what manner they think that the "psychic body" will, by the grace of the resurrection, be changed and become "spiritual;" and in what manner they think that what is sown "in dishonor" is to "rise in glory," and what is sown "in corruption" is to be transformed into "incorruption." Certainly if they believe the Apostle, who says that the body, when it rises in glory and in power and in incorruptibility, has already become spiritual, it seems absurd and contrary to the meaning of the Apostle to say that it is still entangled in the passions of flesh and blood.

Origen's emphatic denial of a physical understanding of the resurrection is especially interesting for two reasons.

First, his confidence in the assertion attests the strength of his conviction that such an understanding is "low and mean:" the problem is not that physical resurrection is unbelievable, but that the conception is unworthy of the hope that faith relates to. Origen's argument presupposes, of course, that a physical understanding of the resurrection was current in Christian Alexandria. But he insists, again following Paul's analysis, that the body which is raised in resurrection is continuous with the physical body in principle, but different from it in substance (*On First Principles,* 2.10.3):

So our bodies should be supposed to fall like a grain of wheat into the earth, but implanted in them is the cause that maintains the essence of the body. Although the bodies die and are corrupted and scattered, nevertheless by the word of God that same cause that has all along been safe in the essence of the body raises them up from the earth and restores and refashions them, just as the power that exists in a grain of wheat refashions and restores the grain, after its corruption and death, into a body with stalk and ear. And so in the case of those who shall be counted worthy of obtaining an inheritance in the kingdom of heaven, the cause before mentioned, by which the body is refashioned, at the order of God refashions out of the earthly and animate body a spiritual body, which can dwell in heaven.

The direction and orientation of Origen's analysis is defined by his concern to describe what in humanity may be regarded as ultimately compatible with the divine. For that reason, physical survival is rejected as an adequate category for explaining the resurrection. Instead, he emphasizes the change of substance that must be involved.

Second, the force behind Origen's assertion is categorical. The resolution of the stated contradictions — "psychic"/"spiritual," "dishonor"/ "glory," "corruption"/"incorruption" — involves taking Paul's language as directly applicable to the human condition. In the case of each contradiction, the first item in the pair needs to yield to the spiritual progression of the second item in the pair. That is the progressive logic of Origen's thought, now applied comprehensively to human experience.

In Origen's articulation, progressive thinking insists upon the radical transition which resurrection involves. Although his discussion is a brilliant exegesis of Paul's argument, Origen also elevates the progressive principle above any other consideration which Paul introduces. Paul had used this kind of method for understanding Scripture (see Gal. 4:21–31), but in Origen's thought that approach is turned into the fundamental principle of global spiritual revolution. Only that, in his mind, can do justice to the promise of being raised from the dead.

For all that the transition from flesh to spirit is radical, Origen is also clear that personal continuity is involved. To put the matter positively, one is clothed bodily with one's own body, as we have already seen. To put the matter negatively, sins borne by the body of flesh may be thought of us visited upon the body which is raised from the dead (*On First Principles*, 2.10.8):

... just as the saints will receive back the very bodies in which they have lived in holiness and purity during their stay in the habitations of this life, but bright and glorious as a result of the resurrection, so, too, the impious, who in this life have loved the darkness of error and the night of ignorance will after the resurrection be clothed with murky and black bodies, in order that this very gloom of ignorance, which in the present world has taken possession of the inner parts of their mind, may in the world to come be revealed through the garment of their outward body.

Although Origen is quite consciously engaging in speculation at this point, he firmly rejects the notion that the flesh is involved in the resurrection, even when biblical promises appear to envisage earthly joys (*On First Principles*, 2.11.2):

Now some people, who reject the labor of thinking and seek after the outward and literal meaning of the law, or rather give way to their own desires and lusts, disciples of the mere letter, consider that the promises of the future are to be looked for in the form of pleasure and bodily luxury. And chiefly on this account they desire after the resurrection to have flesh of such a sort that they will never lack the power to eat and drink and to do all things that pertain to flesh and blood, not following the teaching of the apostle Paul about the resurrection of a "spiritual body."

His reasons for rejecting such a millenarian view are both exegetical and theological. Paul is the ground of the apostolic authority he invokes, in a reading we have already seen. He uses that perspective to consider the Scriptures generally (*On First Principles*, 2.11.3). But Origen deepens his argument from interpretation with a profoundly theological argument. He maintains that the most urgent longing is the desire "to learn the design of those things which we perceive to have been made by God." This longing is as basic to our minds as the eye is to the body: constitutionally, we long for the vision of God (*On First Principles*, 2.11.4).

The manner in which Origen develops his own thought is complex, involving a notion of education in paradise prior to one's entry into the realm of heaven proper (*On First Principles*, 2.11.6):

I think that the saints when they depart from this life will remain in some place situated on the earth, which the divine Scripture calls "paradise." This will be a place of learning and, so to speak, a lecture room or school for souls, in which they may be taught about all that they had seen on earth and may also receive some indication of what is to follow in the future. Just as when placed in this life they had obtained certain indications of the future, seen indeed "through a glass darkly," and yet truly seen "in part," they are revealed more openly and clearly to the saints in the proper places and times. If anyone is of truly pure heart and of clean mind and well-trained understanding he will make swifter progress and quickly ascend to the region of the air,[29] until he reaches the Kingdom of heaven, passing through the series of those "mansions," if I may so call them, which the Greeks have termed spheres — that is, globes — but which the divine Scripture calls heavens.

Even this brief excerpt from a convoluted description represents the complexity of Origen's vision, but two factors remain plain and simple. First, the vision of God is the moving element through the entire discussion. Second, Origen clearly represents and develops a construction of the Christian faith in which eschatology has been swallowed up in an emphasis upon transcendence. The only time which truly matters is that time until one's person death, which determines one's experience in paradise and in the resurrection. "Heaven" as cosmographic place now occupies the central position once occupied by the eschatological kingdom of God in Jesus' teaching. That, too, occurs on the authority of progressive dialectics, the refinement of Pauline metaphysics.

Augustine and the Substance of Resurrection

Unlike Origin, Augustine refutes the Manichaean philosophy which he accepted prior to his conversion to Christianity. In Manichaeanism, named after a Persian teacher of the third century named Mani, light and darkness are two eternal substances which struggle against one another, and they war over the creation they have both participated in making.[30] As in the case of Gnosticism, on which it was dependent, Manichaeanism counseled a denial of the flesh. By his insistence on the resurrection of the flesh, Augustine revives the strong assertion of the

---

29. At this point, Origen is reading 1 Thessalonians 4 through the lens of 1 Corinthians 15, just as later in the passage he incorporates the language of "mansions" from John 14:2.

30. See Stanley Romaine Hopper, "The Anti-Manichean Writings," *A Companion to the Study of St. Augustine* (ed. R. W. Battenhouse; New York: Oxford University Press, 1969) 148–174.

extent of God's embrace of his own creation (in the tradition of Irenaeus, the great millenarian thinker of the second century).[31]

At the same time, Augustine sets a limit on the extent to which one might have recourse to Plato. Augustine had insisted with Plato against the Manichaeans that God was not a material substance, but transcendent. Consequently, evil became in his mind the denial of what proceeds from God (see *Confessions*, 5.10.20). When it came to the creation of people, however, Augustine insisted against Platonic thought that no division between soul and flesh could be made (so *City of God*, 22.12). Enfleshed humanity was the only genuine humanity, and God in Christ was engaged to raise those who were of the city of God. Moreover, Augustine specifically refuted the contention of Porphyry (and Origen) that cycles of creation could be included within the entire scheme of salvation. For Augustine, the power of the resurrection within the world was already confirmed by the miracles wrought by Christ and his martyrs. He gives the example of the healings connected with the relics of St. Stephen, recently transferred to Hippo (*City of God*, 22.8).

Even now, in the power of the Catholic Church, God is represented on earth, and the present Christian epoch (*Christiana tempora*) corresponds to the millennium promised in Revelation 20 (*City of God*, 20.9). This age of dawning power, released in flesh by Jesus and conveyed by the Church, simply awaits the full transition into the city of God, complete with flesh itself. It is telling that, where Origen could cite a saying of Jesus to confirm his view of the resurrection (see Matt. 22:30; Mark 12:25; Luke 20:36), Augustine has to qualify the meaning of the same saying (*City of God*, 22.18):

> They will be equal to angels in immortality and happiness, not in flesh, nor indeed in resurrection, which the angels had no need of, since they could not die. So the Lord said that there would be no marriage in the resurrection, not that there would be no women.

In all of this, Augustine is straining, although he is usually a less convoluted interpreter of Scripture. But he is committed to what the Latin version of the Apostles' Creed promises: "the resurrection of the flesh" and all that implies. He therefore cannot follow Origen's exegesis.

There is a double irony here. First, Origen the sophisticated allegorist seems much simpler to follow in his exegesis of Jesus' teaching than

---

31. See Jaroslav Pelikan, *The Christian Tradition. A History of the Development of Doctrine 1: The Emergence of the Catholic Tradition (100–600)* (Chicago: University of Chicago Press, 1971) 123–132.

Augustine, the incomparable preacher. Second, Augustine's discussion of such issues as the fate of fetuses in the resurrection sounds remarkably like the Sadducees' hypothesis which Jesus argues against in the relevant passage from the Synoptic Gospels.

Augustine is well aware, as was Origen before him, that Paul speaks of a "spiritual body," and acknowledges that "I suspect that all utterance published concerning it is rash." And yet he can be quite categorical that flesh must be involved somehow: "The spiritual flesh will be subject to spirit, but it will still be flesh, not spirit; just as the carnal spirit was subject to the flesh, but was still spirit, not flesh" (*City of God*, 22.21). Such is Augustine's conviction that flesh has become the medium of salvation now and hereafter.

Conclusion

Not only within the New Testament, but through the centuries of discussion which the key figures cited here reflect, Christianity represents itself as a religion of human regeneration. Humanity is regarded, not simply as a quality which God values, but as the very center of human being in the image of God. That center is so precious to God, it is the basis upon which it is possible for human beings to enter the kingdom of God, both now and eschatologically.

The medium in which that ultimate transformation is to take place is a matter of debate. Regenerated people might be compared to angels (so Jesus), to Jesus in his resurrection (so Paul), to spiritual bodies (so Origen), and to spiritualized flesh (so Augustine). But in all of these analyses of how we are to be transformed into the image of Christ so as to apprehend that humanity which is in the image and likeness of God (see Gen. 1:27), there is a fundamental consensus. Jesus is claimed as the agency by which this transformation is accomplished, and its achievement means a profound shift in the very medium in which we are human.

FIVE

The Last Act of Service: Martyrdom for the Torah

The hour at which they brought Rabbi Aqiba out to be put to death was the time for reciting the *Shema*. They were combing his flesh with iron combs while he was accepting upon himself the yoke of the Kingdom of Heaven [in the recitation of the *Shema* — "Hear O Israel, the Lord our God, the Lord is one"].

His disciples said to him, "Our master, to such an extent?"

He said to them, "For my whole life I have been troubled about this verse, 'With all your soul' [meaning] even though he takes your soul. I wondered when I shall have the privilege of carrying out this commandment. Now that it has come to hand, should I not carry it out?"

He held on to the word, "One," until his soul expired [as he said the word] "one." An echo came forth and said, "Happy are you, Rabbi Aqiba, that your soul expired with the word 'one.'"

— BAVLI BERAKHOT 9:1–5 XVIII.1/61B

In the Torah, the Hebrew words for giving one's life for God made known in the Torah are, *qiddush hashem*, meaning "sanctification of the holy name of God." Aqiba's death, which we shall follow in detail later on, embodies the sanctification of God's name: the explicit acceptance of death for the sake of God. Aqiba understands his ordeal in exactly those terms: "with all your soul" meaning "even if he takes your soul." So martyrdom represents a very special kind of death, one that in public bears witness to the martyr's ultimate offering on God's altar: his or her very life. Then the opposite of martyrdom in the Torah is *hillul hashem*, "the profanation of God's holy name." When rabbis who present themselves as embodiments of the Torah cheat or steal, that represents a public disgrace of God. When pious Israelites — faithful Jews — prove

92

more punctilious about what goes into their mouths than what comes out, that, too, represents a *hillul hashem,* as masters of the faith have taught for many centuries.

When we speak of "martyrdom" in English, therefore, we tend to treat the moment as personal and private: the individual's gift of his or her life for God's sake. That stands for an individual's act of bearing witness. But when we use the language of *qiddush hashem,* sanctification of God's name, in the Torah not only the individual is engaged, but the fate and faith of the entirety of holy Israel come into play. The individual sanctifies God's name in public, in the presence of all Israel and humanity beyond. Nothing personal marks the act as idiosyncratic; rather, the act is meant to typify the faith of holy Israel, Israel's acceptance of God's rule even to the very end.

So at stake in *qiddush hashem* or martyrdom in the classical writings of Judaism is the ultimate joining of holy Israel and the private person in the act of sanctifying God's name. Then the individual gives his life for the Torah shared by all. But while individuals enjoy the option of whether or not to give in, by definition the community as a whole does not have the option of changing their private situation, improving it by joining the idolators. All Israel endures eternally — that is the promise of God to Abraham, repeated through the ages by prophets and sages and, to this moment, confirmed by the actualities of history, so far as human time may speak of eternity. And so it is to the individual that the alternative is presented by idolators of good will: join us and we shall treat you well. But all Israel sanctifies God's name in the here and now through not its death but its life within the Torah, the life of sanctification of the here and now embodied in acts of piety and Torah-study.

Here we see the way in which, in a reading of verses of Scripture, the Torah recapitulates accepting death for God's sake. The verse is Song of Songs 6:13: "Return, return, O Shulammite, return, return that we may look upon you. Why should you look upon the Shulammite, as upon a dance before two armies?" The passage commences by identifying the operative clause:

"Return that we may look upon you."

The cited verse, "Return that we may look upon you," is now read as a statement of the idolators to Israel:

The nations of the world say to Israel, "How long are you going to die for your God and devote yourselves completely to him?" "For thus Scripture says, 'Therefore do they love you beyond death' (Song 1:3).

"And how long will you be slaughtered on his account: 'No, but for your sake we are killed all day long' (Ps. 44:23)?

"How long are you going to do good deeds on his account, for him alone, while he pays you back with bad things?

"Come over to us, and we shall make you governors, hyparchs, and generals,

" 'That we may look upon you:' and you will be the cynosure of the world: 'And you shall be the look out of all the people' (Exod. 18:21)."

So is set forth the gentile challenge. It underscores that Israel always has the opportunity of improving its condition in the world. "Join us" and we shall make you rulers. Until the twentieth century, Israelites — if, by definition, not all Israel — had the possibility of accepting the dominant religion, whether Islam or Christianity, and removing from themselves the disabilities, or worse, that the loyalty to the Torah imposed. Indeed, in the massacres that accompanied the Crusades in the Rhineland and else-where in 1096, Jews offered the choice of baptism or drowning killed not only themselves but their children, in the sanctification of God's name. When secular ideologies translated holy Israel into "the Jews," then "Jew" became indelible, and death without alternative the sole result. Within Islam and Christendom, such a possibility defied imagining.

Now returning to our account, we witness the Israelite response:

And the Israelites will answer, "Why should you look upon the Shulammite, as upon a dance before two armies?"

The response follows: Israel is Israel by reason of its loyalty to God and rejection of idolatry. To be Israel means to adhere to the Torah and to the God made manifest therein. As usual, Scripture's facts are systematized and formed into general rules, as the philosophical sages transform Scrip-ture into natural philosophy. That means we take a case and turn it into a rule, an example into a generalization. Hence the matter of the dance:

"In your entire lives, have you ever heard that Abraham, Isaac, and Jacob worshipped idols, that their children should do so after them? Our fathers did not worship idols, and we shall not worship idols after them. But what can you do for us? Can it be like the dance that was made for Jacob, our father, when he went forth from the house of Laban?"

We now turn to instances of Israel's redemption, at the sea and in the time of Elisha:

> "Or can you make a dance for us such as was made for our fathers at the sea? 'And the angel of God removed . . . ' (Exod. 14:19). Or can you make a dance for us like the one that was made for Elisha: 'And when the servant of the man of God was risen early and gone forth, behold a host with horses and chariots was round about the city.' And his servant said to him, 'Alas, my master, what shall we do?' And he answered, 'Do not be afraid, for they who are with us are more than those who are with them.' Forthwith Elisha prayed and said, 'Lord, I pray you, open his eyes that he may see.' And the Lord opened the eyes of the young man, and he saw, and behold, the mountain was full of horses and chariots of fire around about Elisha" (2 Kings 6:15).

And finally comes the end-time, to which the gentiles will not come anyhow:

> "Or can you make a dance for us like the one that the Holy One, blessed be He, will make for the righteous in the age to come?"
> — SONG OF SONGS RABBAH LXXXIX:I.9, 11–12

The passage continues with the exposition of God at the last as Lord of the dance. The question confronts individuals, as the dance or as death is a most private act: How long are you going to die for your God and give him the last full measure of devotion? And there is no dance without individual dancers. But death is public, and there also is no dance without a shared rhythm and gesture. The problem carries along its own solution: At the end of time the individual Israelite joins all Israel in the eschatological dance to be lead by the Lord of the dance, God himself. Here then we find a fine metaphor to make the systematic statement of the problem of evil formulated in both communal and individual terms: Each dancer dances on his own, but all do the same step, stamping together in the same rhythm — predictably, within this theological system, with God leading the way.

Sanctifying God's name engages God with the individual who thereby distinguishes himself or herself. That explains why God will preserve the name of one who is prepared to accept martyrdom to sanctify God's name, that is, for a divine commandment:

> Another interpretation of the verse, "If I should write for him the larger part of my Torah, then he would have been seen as a stranger"

(Hos. 8:12): This is one of the three matters for which Moses was prepared to give his life, on account of which the Holy One, blessed be He, gave them in his name [in line with the sense of the verse, "I should write for him, meaning, in his name"]. The three are the rule of justice, the Torah, and the building of the tabernacle in the wilderness.

Now scriptural facts are ordered to sustain the stated general rule:

How do we know that that is so of the Torah: "Remember the Torah of Moses, my servant" (Mal. 3:22).

The rule of justice: "Moses the lawgiver . . . maintained the righteous judgments of the Lord and his ordinances among Israel" (Deut. 33:21).

How do we know that Moses was prepared to give his life for the sake of the tabernacle:

Rabbi Hiyya ben Joseph said, "On each of the seven days of the consecration of the tabernacle, Moses would dismantle the tabernacle twice a day and then set it up again [thus, morning and evening, for the obligatory daily whole-offering done twice a day]."

Rabbi Hanina the Elder said, "Three times a day he would dismantle it and then erect it."

And should you suppose that someone of the tribe of Levi would give him a hand, our masters have said, "He by himself would dismantle it, and no person of Israel helped him in any way."

Now comes secondary amplification of the point:

"How [do we know that Moses did it by himself]? As it is said, 'And it came to pass on the day that Moses completed setting up the Tabernacle, [he anointed and consecrated it; he also anointed and consecrated its equipment, and the altar and its vessels. The chief men of Israel, heads of families, that is, the chiefs of the tribes who had assisted in preparing the detailed lists, came forward and brought their offering before the Lord]' (Num. 7:1–2). [All that the others did was make the lists and then give their own offering. Moses did the rest.]"

— Pesiqta Rabbati V:II.1

The match now is between eternal life — a name endures — and willingness to give up life. That for which one is prepared to give his life secures for him an enduring name. The principle of rational balance —

you get what you give — is then established by facts of Scripture. Then just as sages insist, "A name made great is a name destroyed" (Tractate Abot 1:13), so they maintain, a life surrendered to God is a life recognized by God.

That is why martyrdom by definition takes place before witnesses. In this respect *qiddush hashem* encompasses "bearing witness," in the Greek and Christian sense of the word. One must accept martyrdom in public and may not expect a miracle to be done on such an occasion; miracles are done only on worthy occasions. But God exacts vengeance for the blood of the martyrs:

> "And you shall not profane [my holy name]:" I derive the implication from the statement, "you shall not profane," that sanctification is covered. And when Scripture says, "but I will be hallowed," the sense is, "Give yourself and sanctify my name." Might one suppose that that is when one is all alone? Scripture says, "among the people of Israel."

Martyrdom takes place in public, because the martyr sanctifies God's name in this world and in this life, and, in line with the language of the liturgy, "We sanctify your Name in public." Just as, in prayer, what follows is the declaration of God's holiness, so, in the crisis of martyrdom, the martyr by his or her deed does the same. But the martyr cannot hold back, expecting a miracle to climax the moment:

> In this connection sages have said: "Whoever gives his life on condition that a miracle is done for him — no miracle will be done for him. But if it is not on condition that a miracle be done for him, a miracle will be done for him."

The pertinent case involves the martyrs who were saved, Hananiah, Mishael, and Azariah, who offered their lives for the sanctification of God's name:

> For so we find in the case of Hananiah, Mishael, and Azariah, that they said to Nebuchadnezzar, "We have no need to answer you in this matter, for if so it must be, our God whom we serve is able to save us from the burning fiery furnace, and he will save us from your power, O king. But even if he does not, be it known to you, O king, that we will not serve your god or worship the statue of gold that you have set up" (Dan. 3:16–18).

And when Marianos seized Pappos and Lulianos, brothers in Laodicea, he said to them, "If you come from the people of Hananiah, Mishael, and Azariah, let your God come and save you from my power."

They said to him, "Hananiah, Mishael, and Azariah were worthy men, and Nebuchadnezzar was a king worthy of having a miracle done on his account.

"But you are a wicked king, and you are not worthy of having a miracle done on your account, and, for our part, we are liable to the death penalty inflicted by Heaven, so if you do not kill us, there are plenty of agents of punishment before the Omnipresent, plenty of bears, plenty of lions, plenty of panthers, plenty of fiery snakes, plenty of scorpions, to do injury to us.

"But in the end the Omnipresent is going to demand the penalty of our blood from your hand."

They say that he did not leave there before orders came from Rome, and they chopped off his head with axes.

Not surprisingly, holy Israel finds its definition in the stipulation that, if the hour calls, Israelites accept martyrdom:

"Who brought you out of the land of Egypt:

"I brought you out of the land of Egypt on a stipulation that you be prepared to give yourselves to sanctify my name."

> "I to be your God":
> like it or not.
> "I am the Lord":
> "I am faithful to pay a reward."
> — Sifra CCXXVII:I.4–8

What is explained is the right attitude for martyrdom. It is one that accepts death for the sake of sanctifying God's name, without the expectation that God will intervene with a miracle. Further, why does God intervene sometimes but not others? That, too, is given a reasonable explanation.

When sages expound the Ten Commandments, therefore, they find among them the requirement that Israel choose martyrdom over the possibility of profaning God's holy name. The pertinent commandment then is the second, "You shall have no other Gods before me." The first, "I am the Lord your God who brought you out of the land of Egypt, out of the house of bondage," is understood to represent the commandment to accept God's rule and dominion. Then comes "You shall have no other Gods." Here is how sages link God's dominion to martyrdom:

"You shall have no other Gods before me" (Exod. 20:3):

Why is this stated?

Since it says, "I am the Lord your God."

The matter may be compared to the case of mortal king who came to a town. His staff said to him, "Issue decrees for them."

He said to them, "No. When they accept my dominion, then I shall issue decrees over them. For if they do not accept my dominion, how are they going to carry out my decrees?"

So said the Omnipresent to Israel, "I am the Lord your God.

"You shall have no other Gods before me.

"I am the one whose dominion you accepted upon yourselves in Egypt."

They said to him, "Indeed so."

"And just as you accepted my dominion upon yourself, now accept my decrees: 'You shall have no other gods before me.'"

If faced with idolatry or death, choose death. Here the matter is brought down to earth:

["The Lord spoke to Moses saying, 'Speak to the Israelite people and say to them, I am the Lord your God'" (Lev. 18:2):]

Rabbi Simeon ben Yohai says, "That is in line with what is said elsewhere: 'I am the Lord your God [who brought you out of the land of Egypt, out of the house of bondage]' (Exod. 20:2).

"'Am I the Lord, whose sovereignty you took upon yourself in Sinai?'

"They said to him, 'Indeed.'

"'And just as you accepted my dominion upon yourself, now accept my decrees.'"

"'You shall not copy the practices of the land of Egypt where you dwelt, or of the land of Canaan to which I am taking you; nor shall you follow their laws.'

"What is said here? 'I am the Lord your God [who brought you out of the land of Egypt, out of the house of bondage]' (Exod. 20:2).

"'Am I the Lord, whose sovereignty you took upon yourself?'

"They said to him, 'Indeed.'

"'And just as you accepted my dominion upon yourself, now accept my decrees.'"

"You shall have no other gods before me" (Exod. 20:3).

"You shall have [no other gods before me]" (Exod. 20:3):

Why is this stated?

Because it is said, "You shall not make for yourself a graven image [or any likeness of anything that is in heaven above, or that is in the earth beneath, or that is in the water under the earth; you shall not bow down to them or serve them]."

I know only that one may not make them. How do I know that as to one that is already made, one may not keep it?

Scripture says, "You shall have [no other gods before me]" (Exod. 20:3).

Now we move on to the matter of martyrdom:

"For I the Lord your God am a jealous God, visiting the iniquity of the fathers upon the children... those who love me and keep my commandments":

"Those who love me" refers to Abraham, our patriarch, and those who are like him.

"And who keep my commandments" refers to the prophets and elders.

The martyrs are explicit. In the time of the sages represented by these teachings, a rebellion against Rome in the Land of Israel, led by a general, Bar Kokhba, in 132–135 C.E. disrupted Roman rule at the very height of its imperial power in the Near East. Regarding the practice of Judaism as the cause, for a brief period — perhaps a decade — the Romans forbade the commandments and the study of the Torah as well. In due course they reestablished a Jewish government under a sage prepared to keep the peace, and the sages themselves produced the laws embodied in the Mishnah and related traditions that were enforced by that regime.

But in the interim it was dangerous to practice Judaism, so the following account, preserved in a document from much later times, alleges:

Rabbi Nathan says, "'Those who love me and keep my commandments' refers to those who dwell in the land of Israel and give their lives for keeping the religious duties.

"'How come you are going forth to be put to death?' 'Because I circumcised my son as an Israelite.'

"'How come you are going forth to be burned to death?' 'Because I read in the Torah.'

" 'How come you are going forth to be crucified?' 'Because I ate unleavened bread.'

" 'How come you are going to be given a hundred lashes?' 'Because I took up the palm branch [on Tabernacles].'

" 'Those with which I was wounded in the house of friends' (Zech. 13:6): these are the wounds that made me beloved to my father who is in heaven."

— MEKHILTA ATTRIBUTED TO R. ISHMAEL LII:I.1

Here is a classical account of specific actions people took to sanctify God's name — commandments or religious duties, performed with the sanctifying blessing, "Blessed are you, Lord our God, king of the world, who has sanctified us by his commandments and commanded us to...," followed by the specification of the act, e.g., circumcision, declaiming the Torah, eating unleavened bread on Passover, taking up the palm branch on the Festival of Tabernacles.

But among all actions by which God's name is sanctified, Torah-study takes pride of place, as we saw in Chapter One. We cannot find surprising, therefore, that Torah-study provided the occasion for the single most remarkable story of martyrdom set forth in the entirety of classical Rabbinic writings, the martyrdom of Aqiba, to which reference was made at the beginning of this chapter. To understand the story, we have to take it up in the context in which it is told. That is set by the statement of the Mishnah:

A person is obligated to recite a blessing over evil just as he recites a blessing over good, as it is said, "And you shall love the Lord your God with all your heart, with all your soul and with all your might" (Deut. 6:5).

"With all your heart" — [this means] with both of your inclinations, with the good inclination and with the evil inclination.

"And with all your soul" — even if He takes your soul.

"And with all your might" — with all of your money.

Another matter: "With all your might" — with each and every measure that he measures out for you, thank him much.

— MISHNAH-TRACTATE BERAKHOT 9:5

The cited verse takes its place in prayer; after the proclamation of God's unity and dominion, the worshipper then says, "And you shall love...." Now sages take up the exposition of that matter:

"You shall love the Lord your God":

It has been taught on Tannaite authority:

Rabbi Eliezer says, "If it is said, 'With all your soul,' why is it also said, 'With all your might'? And if it is said, 'With all your might,' why is it also said, 'With all your soul'? But if there is someone who places greater value on his body than on his possessions, for such a one it is said, 'With all your soul.'

"And if there is someone who places greater value on his possessions than on his life, for such a one it is said, 'With all your might.' "

Rabbi Aqiba says, " 'With all your soul' — even if he takes your soul."

Now the teaching of Aqiba is re-presented as a dramatic story:

Our rabbis have taught on Tannaite authority:

The wicked government once made a decree that the Israelites should not take up the study of Torah.

"The wicked government" refers to Rome, and the setting, as we noted, is the repression following the war led by Bar Kokhba. Not everyone followed the model of "those who suffered wounds to be beloved by my Father in heaven," and among those who took a conciliatory position is Pappos ben Judah, that is, a Jew with a Roman personal name, but an Israelite father:

Pappos ben Judah came and found Rabbi Aqiba gathering crowds in public and taking up the study of Torah.

He said to him, "Aqiba, aren't you afraid of the government?"

He said to him, "I shall show you a parable. What is the matter like? It is like the case of a fox who was going along the river and saw fish running in swarms place to place."

"He said to them, 'Why are you running away?' "

"They said to him, 'Because of the nets people cast over us.' "

"He said to them, 'Why don't you come up on dry land, and you and I can live in peace as my ancestors lived in peace with yours?' "

"They said to him, 'Are you the one they call the cleverest of all wild beasts? You are not clever, you're a fool. Now if in the place in which we can live, we are afraid, in a place in which we perish, how much the more so [should we fear]!' "

"Now we too, if when we are in session and taking up the study of Torah, in which it is written, 'For it is your life and the length of your days' (Deut. 30:20), things are as they are, if we should go and abandon it, how much the more so [shall we be in trouble]!"

Aqiba was arrested, but so was Pappos:

> They say that only a few days passed before they arrested and imprisoned Rabbi Aqiba. They arrested and imprisoned Pappos ben Judah nearby. He said to him, "Pappos, who brought you here?" He said to him, "Happy are you, Aqiba, because you were arrested on account of teachings of Torah. Woe is Pappos, who was arrested on account of nonsense."

Aqiba was executed early in the morning, at the time for reciting the Shema and thereby accepting the dominion of Heaven for oneself:

> The hour at which they brought Rabbi Aqiba out to be put to death was the time for reciting the Shema. They were combing his flesh with iron combs while he was accepting upon himself [in the recitation of the Shema] the yoke of the Kingdom of Heaven.

That at such a moment Aqiba recited the Shema astonished his disciples, among the bystanders:

> His disciples said to him, "Our master, to such an extent?"
> He said to them, "For my whole life I have been troubled about this verse, 'With all your soul' [meaning] even though he takes your soul. I wondered when I shall have the privilege of carrying out this commandment. Now that it has come to hand, should I not carry it out?"
> He held on to the word, "One," until his soul expired [as he said the word] "one." An echo came forth and said, "Happy are you, Rabbi Aqiba, that your soul expired with the word 'one.'"
> The serving angels said before the Holy One, blessed be He, "Is this Torah and that the reward? 'From them that die by your hand, O Lord' (Ps. 17:14) [ought to have been his lot]."
> He said to them, "'Their portion is in life' (Ps. 17:14)."
> An echo went forth and proclaimed, "Happy are you, R. Aqiba, for you are selected for the life of the world to come."
> — BAVLI BERAKHOT 9:1–5 XVIII.1/61B

Aqiba's death then raised the question of theodicy: How could an all-powerful and loving God permit the exemplary master of the Torah to suffer and die in such a way? That is a natural question for monotheism.

For, we realize, while a religion of numerous gods finds many solutions to one problem, a religion of only one God presents one to many. Life is seldom fair. Rules rarely work. To explain the reason why, polytheisms adduce multiple causes of chaos, a god per anomaly. Diverse gods do various things, so, it stands to reason, ordinarily outcomes conflict. Monotheism by nature explains many things in a single way. One God rules. Life is meant to be fair, and just rules are supposed to describe what is ordinary, all in the name of that one and only God. So in monotheism a simple logic governs to limit ways of making sense of things. But that logic contains its own dialectics. If one true God has done everything, then, since he is God all-powerful and omniscient, all things are credited to, and blamed on, him. In that case he can be either good or bad, just or unjust — but not both. And the martyrdom of Aqiba set the occasion for asking that question that is natural to monotheism: Why did God permit such a thing? Here is the answer, once more in the form of a story:

> Said Rabbi Judah, "At the time that Moses went up on high, he found the Holy One in session, affixing crowns to the letters [of the words of the Torah]. He said to him, 'Lord of the universe, who is stopping you [from regarding the document as perfect without these additional crowns on the letters]?'
>
> "He said to him, 'There is a man who is going to arrive at the end of many generations, and Aqiba ben Joseph is his name, who is going to interpret on the basis of each point of the crowns heaps and heaps of laws.'
>
> "He said to him, 'Lord of the Universe, show him to me.'
>
> "He said to him, 'Turn around.'
>
> "He went and took a seat at the end of eight rows, but he could not grasp what the people were saying. He felt faint. But when the discourse reached a certain matter, and the disciples said, 'My lord, how do you know this?' and he answered, 'It is a law given to Moses from Sinai,' he regained his composure.
>
> "He went and came before the Holy One. He said before him, 'Lord of the Universe, How come you have someone like that and yet you give the Torah through me?'
>
> "He said to him, 'Silence! That is how the thought came to me.'
>
> "He said to him, 'Lord of the Universe, you have shown me his Torah, now show me his reward.'
>
> "He said to him, 'Turn around.'

"He turned around and saw his flesh being weighed out at the butcher-stalls in the market.

"He said to him, 'Lord of the Universe, Such is Torah, such is the reward?'

"He said to him, 'Silence! That is how the thought came to me.'"

— B. MEN. 3:7 II.5/29A–B

To understand the enchanted world in which such a story can be told, we recall that, for sages, the Torah is not a history book with a beginning, middle, and end, and time has no bearing on events. They say, "Considerations of temporal order do not apply to the Torah," meaning, the rigid division of past, present, and future does not apply. Moses and Aqiba take positions within a single plane of time. That is why Moses, who embodies humility for holy Israel, can ask God why God chose Moses as the medium of the Torah, when he had so much more able a choice in Aqiba. Moses could not aspire to the intellectual power of Aqiba, but when Aqiba attributed his findings to the logic initiated by Moses, he was appeased. But then, seeing the reward for Aqiba's great accomplishments in the Torah, Moses asked the question that is natural to monotheism. And he got the brutally honest answer: "Silence! That is my decree."

Such an answer could not persuade everybody. That God in the end transcended even the rationality of the Torah, with its insistence — also set forth in the Shema — that if Israel obeyed God with humility, God would restore Israel to the Land, meaning, Adam and Eve to Eden. So not everything can be explained, and many things cannot. But, alongside, sages wanted logical explanations for their fates. Other sages fell victim to the repression that followed the war against Rome, and of some of these the story is told that they wanted to know what they had done wrong to merit the fate they now suffered. Martyrdom represents an opportunity to serve God, but not one that the Israelite is required to seek. What troubled sages is that they were put to death like criminals, and they asked what they had done to deserve it. Now the question contains its own answer. The question — "Why are we put to death like those who profane the Sabbath...fornicate...kill?" — bears within itself a certain pride. But pride is the opposite of that humility that the Torah inculcates. The sin of Adam and Eve took place because they set their will against God's, an act of pride attesting to the absence of humility. So here too, we see, martyrdom turns out to punish the sin of pride:

When they seized Rabban Simeon ben Gamaliel and Rabbi Ishmael
on the count of death, Rabban Simeon ben Gamaliel was in session
and was perplexed, saying, "Woe is us! For we are put to death
like those who profane the Sabbath and worship idols and practice
fornication and kill."

Said to him Rabbi Ishmael ben Elisha, "Would it please you if I
said something before you?"

He said to him, "Go ahead."

He said to him, "Is it possible that when you were sitting at a
banquet, poor folk came and stood at your door, and you did not
let them come in and eat?"

He said to him, "By heaven [may I be cursed] if I ever did such
a thing! Rather, I set up guards at the gate. When poor folk came
along, they would bring them in to me and eat and drink with me
and say a blessing for the sake of Heaven."

— The Fathers according to Rabbi Nathan XXXVIII:V.2

So Simeon b. Gamaliel, that is, the scion of the house of the Jewish
government of Israel, that is, the Jews in the Land of Israel in the later
first and second centuries, provided for the poor and did so in an alert
and punctilious way, so that the poor were treated with dignity and
respect. That cannot account for what was happening. But then, if not
neglect of the poor, what is left but pride:

He said to him, "Is it possible that when you were in session and
expounding [the Torah] on the Temple mount and the vast pop-
ulations of Israelites were in session before you, you took pride in
yourself?"

He said to him, "Ishmael my brother, one has to be ready to
accept his failing. [That is why I am being put to death, the pride
that I felt on such an occasion.]"

— The Fathers according to Rabbi Nathan XXXVIII:V.2

Death on its own comes, so the sages did not fear death. On the contrary,
they knew that death marked only a step on the road to resurrection and
eternal life, so death brought no dread. But how one died would matter:

They went on appealing to the executioner for grace. This one
[Ishmael] said to him, "I am a priest, son of a high priest, kill me
first, so that I do not have to witness the death of my companion."

And the other [Simeon] said, "I am the patriarch, son of the patriarch, kill me first, so that I do not have to witness the death of my companion."

He said to him, "Cast lots." They cast lots, and the lot fell on Rabban Simeon ben Gamaliel.

The executioner took the sword and cut off his head.

Rabbi Ishmael ben Elisha took it and held it in his breast and wept and cried out: "Oh holy mouth, oh faithful mouth, oh mouth that brought forth beautiful gems, precious stones and pearls! Who has laid you in the dust, who has filled your mouth with dirt and dust?

"Concerning you Scripture says, 'Awake, O sword, against my shepherd and against the man who is near to me' (Zech. 13:7)."

He had not finished speaking before the executioner took the sword and cut off his head.

Concerning them Scripture says, "My wrath shall wax hot, and I will kill you with the sword, and your wives shall be widows, and your children fatherless"(Exod. 22:23).

— THE FATHERS ACCORDING TO RABBI NATHAN XXXVIII:V.2

Death atones for sin, and Simeon dies secure in the knowledge that, by his death, he has atoned for the sin of pride. Here, martyrdom represents an opportunity to serve God by dying as an act of atonement. That reading of the meaning of the personal sacrifice does not intersect with the account of how Aqiba sanctified God's name. But it also does not run parallel with it. Rather, martyrdom serves to secure for the martyr that reconciliation with God, attained through an act of utter self-abnegation, that promises eternal life. In that context, what counts in the martyrdom is the suffering, and martyrdom is simply another moment of self-sacrifice: to suffer is to enjoy the opportunity for repentance and atonement:

And, furthermore, a person should rejoice in suffering more than in good times. For if someone lives in good times his entire life, he will not be forgiven for such sin as may be in his hand.

And how shall he attain forgiveness? Through suffering.

Rabbi Eliezer ben Jacob says, "Lo, Scripture says, 'For whom the Lord loves he corrects, even as a father corrects the son in whom he delights' (Prov. 3:12).

"What made the son be pleasing to the father? You must say it was suffering [on account of correction]."

Rabbi Meir says, "Lo, Scripture says, 'And you shall consider in your heart, that as a man chasten his son, so the Lord your God chastens you' (Deut. 8:5).

"You know in your heart the deeds that you did, and also the suffering that I brought upon you, which was not in accord with the deeds that you did at all."

Rabbi Yosé ben Rabbi Judah says, "Beloved is suffering, for the name of the Omnipresent rests upon the one upon whom suffering comes, as it is said, 'So the Lord your God chastens you' (Deut. 8:5)."

Rabbi Nathan ben Rabbi Joseph says, "Just as a covenant is made through the land, so a covenant is made through suffering, as it is said, 'The Lord, your God chastens you' (Deut. 8:7).

"And it says, 'For the Lord your God brings you into a good land' (Deut. 8:7)."

Rabbi Simeon ben Yohai says, "Suffering is precious. For through suffering three good gifts were given to Israel, which the nations of the world desire, and these are they: the Torah, the land of Israel, and the world to come.

"How do we know that that is the case for the Torah? As it is said, 'To know wisdom and chastisement' (Prov. 1:2). And it is said, 'Happy is the person whom you chastise O Lord and teach out of your Torah' (Ps. 94:12).

"How do we know that that is the case for the land of Israel? 'The Lord your God chastens you ... for the Lord your God brings you into a good land' (Deut. 8:5, 7).

"How do we know that that is the case for the world to come? 'For the commandment is a lamp and the Torah is a light, and reproofs of chastisement are the way of life' (Prov. 6:23). What is the way that brings a person to the world to come? One must say it is suffering."

Rabbi Nehemiah says, "Beloved is suffering, for just as offerings appease, so does suffering appease.

"In the case of offerings, Scripture says, 'And it shall be accepted for him to make atonement for him' (Lev. 1:4).

"And in the case of suffering: 'And they shall be paid the punishment for their iniquity' (Lev. 26:43).

"And not only so, but suffering appeases more than do offerings. For offerings are a matter of property, but suffering, of one's own body.

"And so Scripture says, 'Skin for skin, yes, all that a man has will he give for his life' (Job 2:4)."
— SIFRÉ TO DEUTERONOMY XXXII:V.5FF.

Suffering by reason of punishment for sin is to be valued, because through suffering one atones. Hence a doctrine of suffering encompasses not only the cause — rebellion — but also what is achieved — humility, yielding repentance. Scripture also represents suffering as divine chastisement and instruction, to be received gratefully. Not only does suffering yield atonement, it also appeases the way offerings do.

Two views of martyrdom, Aqiba's and Simeon's, then set side by side two doctrines of what martyrdom means, both of them focused upon the present moment, on the one side, and the action of the individual representing Israel, on the other. The one portrays martyrdom as the perfect act of love for God, the fulfillment in its most complete form of the commandment to love God with all one's heart, soul, and might. The other finds in martyrdom an act of suffering unto atonement of sin. Both representations of sages' deaths, then, take martyrdom as a chapter in the life of one or another Israelite: Aqiba shows the martyr as saint, Simeon, the martyr as one who atones for sin. But neither story, except by implication, takes up the martyrdom of the entire people, Israel, such as has taken place in one age after another, and, especially, in our own day. And yet, when sages themselves think of "Israel," they think not only of the fate of the individual Israelite but also, and especially, of the entirety of Israel, viewed not only all together, but also in the setting of time and eternity.

Martyrdom takes place within Israel, the holy people, and not only in the setting of the life of the martyr alone. Hence when sages contemplate martyrdom, their minds turn to the condition of all Israel, not the people that produces martyrs, but the martyred people. In this day and age, such language, encompassing an entire community within the category of the martyr, does not exaggerate but understates reality. But sages find in Israel's martyrdom important evidence of Israel's coming redemption and the advent of the world to come. When sages speak of the world to come, their language signifies a final change in relationship between God and humanity, a model of how God and humanity relate that marks the utter restoration of the world order originally contemplated. That is the way humanity and God conduct their cosmic transaction that God had intended from the beginning and for eternity — time having no place in his category-formation for ordering creation. The point, specifically, is that Israel enjoys a set of relationships with God that are not differentiated temporally and certainly not organized in causal patterns of sequence, in ordered, causative sequence through time, but in other ways. Here is how those other ways are delineated:

> Once upon a time Rabban Gamaliel, Rabbi Eleazar ben Azariah, Rabbi Joshua, and Rabbi Aqiba were walking along the way and heard the roar of Rome all the way from Puteoli, at a distance of a hundred and twenty miles. They began to cry, but Rabbi Aqiba brightened up.
>
> They said to him, "Why so cheerful?"
>
> He said to them, "Why so gloomy?"
>
> They said to him, "These Cushites worship sticks and stones and burn incense to idolatry but live in safety and comfort, while as to us, the house that was the footstool for our God is burned with fire! Why shouldn't we cry?!"
>
> He said to them, "But that's precisely why I rejoice. If those who violate his will have it so good, those who do his will all the more so!"
>
> Once again, they were going up to Jerusalem. When they got to Mount Scopus, they tore their garments. When they reached the Temple mount, they saw a fox emerge from the house of the Holy of Holies. They began to cry, but Rabbi Aqiba brightened up.
>
> They said to him, "Why so cheerful?"
>
> He said to them, "Why so gloomy?"
>
> They said to him, "The place of which it once was said, 'And the non-priest who draws near shall be put to death' (Num. 1:51), has become a fox hole, so shouldn't we weep?"
>
> He said to them, "But that's precisely why I rejoice. It is written, 'And I will take to me faithful witnesses to record, Uriah the priest and Zechariah son of Jeberechiah' (Isa. 8:2). And what has Uriah the priest to do with Zechariah? Uriah lived during the first Temple, and Zechariah during the second, but Scripture had linked the prophecy of Zechariah to the prophecy of Uriah. In the case of Uriah: 'Therefore shall Zion for your sake be ploughed as a field' (Mic. 3:12). Zechariah: 'Thus says the Lord of hosts, there shall yet old men and old women sit in the broad places of Jerusalem' (Zech. 8:4). Until the prophecy of Uriah was fulfilled, I was afraid that the prophecy of Zechariah might not be fulfilled. Now that the prophecy of Uriah has come about, we may

be certain that the prophecy of Zechariah will be fulfilled word for word."

They said to him, "Aqiba, you have given us comfort, Aqiba, you have given us comfort."

— BAVLI-TRACTATE MAKKOT 3:16 II.4/24A–B

So here the story comes full circle that commences with God's creation of a perfect world defined by a just order. That world exhibits flaws, it is not perfect by reason of the character of humanity. But the world will be restored to perfection (requiring, then, eternity), humanity to Eden, Israel to the Land of Israel, through humanity's, and Israel's, act of repentance and reconciliation with God. That act of reconciliation, prepared for in countless lives of virtue and acts of merit, is realized in the world or age to come. But it is not only in those lives, but also in the martyrdom suffered by so many, that that reconciliation can take place.

Martyrdom, which defines the very condition of Israel, its life in exile, serves as guarantee of the redemption that God is going to bring about. That relationship of complementarity — oppression, redemption — is why the act of oppression, now realized, validates the hope for the Messiah to signal the advent of the redemption fulfilled in the world to come. The theology not only accommodates the dissonant fact of Israel's martyrdom but finds reassurance in it, as is stated in so many words:

Rabbi Helbo in the name of Rabbi Yohanan said, "Better was the removing of the ring by Pharaoh [for the sealing of decrees to oppress the Israelites] than the forty years during which Moses prophesied concerning them, because it was through this [oppression] that the redemption came about, while through that [prophesying] the redemption did not come about."

Rabbi Simeon ben Laqish said, "Better was the removing of the ring by Ahasuerus decreeing persecution of Israel in Media than the sixty myriads of prophets who prophesied in the days of Elijah, because it was through this [oppression] that the redemption came about, while through that [prophesying] the redemption did not come about."

Rabbis said, "Better was the Book of Lamentations than the forty years in which Jeremiah prophesied over them, because in it the Israelites received full settlement of their iniquities on the day the temple was destroyed.

"That is in line with the following verse: 'The punishment of your iniquity, O daughter of Zion, is accomplished.'"

LAMENTATIONS RABBATI CXXII:I.I

Martyred Israel's future is already clear from its present. Just as the prophetic prediction of the ruin of Jerusalem has been realized, so the same prophets' promises of ultimate salvation will also come about. That yields a certainty about what is going to happen. The whole then forms a coherent pattern, one that reveals what will happen through what has happened. The martyr stands for the entirety of Israel's history, the martyr's ultimate destiny, Israel's divinely planned reward: to live forever. That is what is at stake in martyrdom for the Torah, it is what happens when people sanctify God's name in public: the heart and soul of spirituality in Judaism.

S I X

Imitatio Christi

Beloved, we should love one another, because love is from God, and the one who loves has been begotten from God and knows God. And the one who does not love does not know God, because God is love. By this the love of God is manifested in us, because God sent his unique Son into the world so that we might live through him. In this is love: not that we have loved God, but that he loved us and sent his Son, an appeasement for our sins. Beloved, if God so loved us, we also ought to love one another. No one has ever sighted God. If we love one another, God remains in us and his love has been perfected in us. By this we know that we remain in him and he in us, because he has given from his Spirit.

—1 JOHN 4:7–13

Written just after the dawn of the second century C.E., the first letter of John takes up many of the principal themes of John's Gospel and puts them into the setting of what was then emerging as a universal or catholic Christianity. The passage cited evokes the conclusion of the Gospel's prologue, "No has ever seen God; the one who is in the bosom of the Father, uniquely God, that one has made him known" (John 1:18). The Gospel is focused on the christology of Jesus' status as the incarnational expression of God, subsuming and integrating all other expressions. The first letter of John intends to relate that christology to the communal lives of churches, no matter which of the various apostolic founders they claimed affiliation with. The great Petrine theme of transformation by the Spirit of God is here incorporated within the Johannine theme of the unique expression of the Father by means of the Son.

The result is a simply stated, frequently recapitulated perspective on what has been called the *imitatio Christi*, the imitation of Christ. That is by no means a peculiarly Johannine concept. "Become imitators of me, just as I also am of Christ," is Paul's direct injunction, given with little warning and even less explanation, as if those who heard his letter read in Corinth would know what he meant (1 Cor. 11:1). That is not surprising, when we keep in mind the saying of Jesus (Matt. 11:28–29) which we cited at the opening of Chapter 2. Jesus' relation to God, and the believer's relation to God by means of Jesus, was so basic to Christianity's approach to Spirit, even before it became a movement self-consciously separate from Judaism, that both those relations are often more assumed than explained. Just as John's Gospel takes up the task of explaining Jesus' relation to God, by adapting and complementing the Synoptic Gospels in a considered meditation of the sources and results of the Son's grace and truth, so the first letter of John undertakes a sustained exegesis of the identity of believers in the light of Jesus' identity.

"Beloved, now we are God's children, and it has not yet been manifested what we shall be: we know that when it is manifested, we shall be like him, because we shall see him just as he is" (1 John 3:2). The central insight of the first letter of John is that the *imitatio Christi* is not only an injunction, but the constitutive element of who the people of God are. By the time the letter was written, Christianity had long been defined, in official terms, by means of its illegitimacy.[1] The Roman government no longer saw it as a part of Judaism, and therefore Christians could not claim exemption, as Jews could, from the civic obligation to offer sacrifice to the emperor as God's son. That made for an environment of persecution, frequently official and often violent, as well as aggressive and abusive. Centuries of injury ironically provided the emerging Church with a coherent ethic of exemplary resistance, as well as a publicly recognizable persona, neither of which was a natural result of the highly factional, disorganized movement which the New Testament attests in the first century. But Roman repression was obviously not responsible on its own for making Christianity into the one rival it could not defeat. That policy resulted in the greater coherence of Christianity for the simple reason that the movement had something to be coherent about. The *imitatio Christi* was not the product of persecution, but an environment of persecution made martyrdom the most natural expression of the *imitatio Christi*.

The depth and persistence of the conviction among Christians that their experience related to Jesus', and that Jesus' experience directly related to God's, reveal the awareness of *mimesis* — the Greek point of departure for the notion of *imitatio* in Latin Christianity[2] — operating

---

1. For a discussion, see Bruce Chilton and Jacob Neusner; *Trading Places. The Intersecting Histories of Judaism and Christianity* (Cleveland: Pilgrim, 1996).

2. For a discussion of mimesis, especially in relation to the recent theories of René Girard,

in two directions at once. Divine *mimesis*, identified in 1 John as love, proceeds from God, through Jesus, to the believer. In this way, believers are understood to be "begotten" of God in the sense that Jesus was, as well. At each level — the Father's, the Son's, and believers' — the initial act of God defines the principle of action, but the results of that loving action are unique at each level and in each case. In addition to divine *mimesis*, reaching through Christ to believers, there is also human *mimesis*, moving in the reverse direction and working out human identity by taking the image of God to itself.

The crowning achievement of the Johannine literature within the New Testament, the fourth Gospel and the epistles of John taken together, is the articulation of this double *mimesis* with unparalleled clarity. Yet the reason such clarity was possible, and the basis on which the *imitatio Christi* enjoys such a deep resonance both within the New Testament and in the tradition of Christian spirituality, is that the divine and human *mimesis* is not the invention of any person's or any group's theology, but characterizes features of Christian practice in every age. Appreciating that takes nothing away from the Johannine accomplishment. On the contrary, it serves to specify the particular genius of this seam of New Testament literature: its reach for a catholic consensus indeed enabled Johannine thinkers to bring to word what had largely been a matter of practice, with little or only subliminal awareness.

Over the past ten years, I have developed an account of the development of eucharistic practices within primitive Christianity, beginning with the contributions of Jesus as a conscious practitioner of Judaism. The first book in this direction was *The Temple of Jesus*,[3] in which I engaged explicitly with the work of anthropologists of sacrifice in order to understand Jesus' position in regard to the cultus in Jerusalem. Indeed, eucharist at the time I initially researched the book was not foremost in my mind. My principal concern had been to assess Jesus' attitudes toward and actions in the Temple itself. But in the course of that work, I saw the direct connection between Jesus' last meals with his followers and his action in the Temple. The eucharist emerged, then, as a surrogate of sacrifice. Encouraged by many scholars, notably Bernhard Lang, I then undertook in *A Feast of Meanings*[4] a properly exegetical study, in order

---

see Bruce Chilton, *The Temple of Jesus. His Sacrificial Program within a Cultural History of Sacrifice* (University Park: The Pennsylvania State University Press, 1992).

3. Cited above.

4. Bruce Chilton, *A Feast of Meanings. Eucharistic Theologies from Jesus through Johannine Circles* (NovTSup 72; Leiden: Brill, 1994).

to detail the evolution of the texts within the typical practices of the first Christians. That analytic work, in turn, was presented in a more accessible form, within a religio-historical framework, in *Jesus' Prayer and Jesus' Eucharist.*[5]

Here I wish briefly to explain the types of eucharist — especially as surrogates, metaphors, and sacraments of sacrifice — attested within the New Testament. These practices, it becomes clear, were far from merely incidental: insofar as they emerged out of conscious, practical repetition with an awareness of the meanings involved and the feelings engendered, they reflect a cultic praxis every bit as characteristic as worship in the Temple had once been in early Judaism. Especially as Christian praxis developed metaphorically and sacramentally, the double *mimesis* involved in martyrdom came to the fore, and the foundations of the Johannine expression of a truly catholic Christianity were well and truly justified. But then I wish to return to a theoretical question, in order to be more precise about the moment eucharist emerged as a surrogate of sacrifice within Jesus' practice, because that appears to have been the moment generative of the other types, and of the mimetic system which is characteristic of Christianity in every age.

Introductory

The Mishnah, in an effort to conceive of a heinous defect on the part of a priest involved in slaughtering the red heifer, pictures him as intending to eat the flesh or drink the blood (*Para* 4:3). Because people had no share of blood, which belonged only to God, the thought of drinking it was blasphemous. To imagine drinking human blood, consumed with human flesh, could only make the blasphemy worse. So if Jesus' words are taken with their traditional, autobiographical meaning, his last supper can only be understood as a deliberate break from Judaism. Either Jesus himself promulgated a new religion, or his followers did so in his name, and invented the last supper themselves. Both those alternatives find adherents today among scholars, and the debate between those who see the Gospels as literally true reports and those who see them as literary fictions shows little sign of offering anything like progress. But in either case, the question remains: if the generative act was indeed anti-sacrificial (whether that act was literal or literary), how did the cycles of

---

5. Bruce Chilton, *Jesus' Prayer and Jesus' Eucharist: His Personal Practice of Spirituality* (Valley Forge: Trinity Press International, 1997).

traditions and the texts as they stand come to their present, sacrificial constructions?

There is another, more historical way of understanding how eucharist emerged in earliest Christianity, an approach which takes account of the cultural changes which the development of the movement involved. Interest in the social world of early Judaism, and in how Christianity as a social movement emerged within Judaism and then became distinct from it, has been growing for most of this century. The result is that we are no longer limited to the old dichotomy, between the "conservative" position that the Gospels are literal reports and the "liberal" position that they are literary fictions. Critical study has revealed that the Gospels are composite products of the various social groups which were part of Jesus' movement from its days within Judaism to the emergence of Christianity as a distinct religion. When we place eucharistic practices within the social constituencies which made the Gospels into the texts we can read today, we can understand the original meaning Jesus gave to the last supper, and how his meaning generated others.

The last supper was not the only supper, just the last one.[6] In fact, the last supper would have had no meaning apart from Jesus' well established custom of eating with people socially. There was nothing unusual about a rabbi making social eating an instrument of his instruction, and it was part of Jesus' method from the first days of his movement in Galilee.

Meals within Judaism were regular expressions of social solidarity, and of common identity as the people of God. Many sorts of meals are attested in the literature of early Judaism. From Qumran we learn of banquets at which the community convened in order of hierarchy; from the Pharisees we learn of collegial meals shared within fellowships (*haburoth*) at which like-minded fellows (*haberim*) would share the foods and the company they considered pure. Ordinary households might welcome the coming of the Sabbath with a prayer of sanctification (*kiddush*) over a cup of wine, and open a family occasion with a blessing (*berakhah*) over bread and wine.

Jesus' meals were similar in some ways to several of these meals, but they were also distinctive. He had a characteristic understanding of what the meals meant and of who should participate in them. For him, eating socially with others in Israel was a parable of the feast in the kingdom which was to come. The idea that God would offer festivity for all peoples

---

6. I owe the phrasing to Hershel Shanks, who in private correspondence used it to help summarize my position; see "The Eucharist — Exploring its Origins," *Bible Review* 10.6 (December 1994) 36–43.

on his holy mountain (see Isa. 2:2–4) was a key feature in the fervent expectations of Judaism during the first century, and Jesus was held to have shared that hope at an early stage, as may be seen in a saying from the source of his teaching known as "Q" (see Matt. 8:11 = Luke 13:28–29):

> Many shall come from east and west,
> and feast with Abraham, Isaac, and Jacob
> in the kingdom of God.[7]

Eating was a way of enacting the kingdom of God, of practicing the generous rule of the divine king. As a result, Jesus avoided exclusive practices, which divided the people of God from one another in his view; he was willing to accept as companions people such as tax agents and others of suspect purity, and to receive well-known sinners at table. The meal for him was a sign of the kingdom of God, and all the people of God, assuming they sought forgiveness, were to have access to it.

Jesus' practice of fellowship at meals caused opposition from those whose understanding of Israel was exclusive. To them, he seemed profligate, willing to eat and drink with anyone, as Jesus himself was pictured as observing in a famous saying also from "Q" (Matt. 11:19 = Luke 7:34):

> A man came eating and drinking, and they complained:
> Look, a glutton and drunkard, a fellow of tax agents and sinners.

Some of Jesus' opponents saw the purity of Israel as something which could only be guarded by separating from others, as in the meals of their fellowships (*haburoth*). Jesus' view of purity was different. He held that a son or daughter of Israel, by virtue of being of Israel, could approach his table, or even worship in the Temple. Where necessary, repentance beforehand could be demanded, and Jesus taught his followers to pray for forgiveness daily, but his understanding was that Israelites as such were pure, and were fit to bring their offerings within the sacrificial worship of Israel.

As long as Jesus' activity was limited to Galilee, he was involved in active disputes, but essentially inconsequential ones. (Slightly deviant rabbis in Galilee were far from uncommon.) But Jesus also brought his

---

7. Because my interest here is in the traditional form of the saying, before changes introduced in Matthew and Luke, I give a reconstructed form; see *God in Strength: Jesus' Announcement of the Kingdom*, Studien zum Neuen Testament und seiner Umwelt 1 (Freistadt: Plöchl, 1979); reprinted Biblical Seminar 8 (Sheffield: JSOT Press, 1987) 179–201. More recently, see *Pure Kingdom. Jesus' Vision of God Studying the Historical Jesus 1* (Eerdmans: Grand Rapids and London: SPCK, 1996) 12–14.

teaching into the Temple, where he insisted on his own teaching (or *halakhah*) of purity. The incident which reflects the resulting dispute is usually called the cleansing of the Temple (Mark 11:15–18; compare Matt. 21:12–17 = Luke 19:45–48 = John 2:13–12):

> And they come into Yerushalayim. He entered into the sacred space and began to throw out those who sold and those who bought in the sacred space, and the tables of the exchangers and the seats of the pigeon-sellers he turned over. And he did not let anyone to carry a vessel through the sacred space. And he was teaching and saying, 'Is it not written that: my house shall be called a house of prayer for all the Gentiles? But you have made it a thugs' lair.' And the high priests and the letterers heard, and sought how they could destroy him, because they feared him, because all the crowed were overwhelmed at his teaching.

From the point of view of the authorities there, what Jesus was after was the opposite of cleansing. He objected to the presence of merchants who had been given permission to sell sacrificial animals in the vast, outer court of the Temple. His objection was based on his own, peasant's view of purity: Israel should offer, not priest's produce for which they handed over money, but their own sacrifices which they brought into the Temple. He believed so vehemently what he taught that he and his followers drove the animals and the sellers out of the great court, no doubt with the use of force.[8]

Jesus' interference in the ordinary worship of the Temple might have been sufficient by itself to bring about his execution. After all, the Temple was the center of Judaism for as long as it stood. Roman officials were so interested in its smooth functioning at the hands of the priests whom they appointed that they were known to sanction the penalty of death for sacrilege. Yet there is no indication that Jesus was arrested immediately. Instead, he remained at liberty for some time, and was finally taken into custody just after one of his meals, the last supper. The decision of the authorities of the Temple to move against Jesus when they did is what made the last supper last.

Why did the authorities wait, and why did they act when they did? The Gospels portray them as fearful of the popular backing which Jesus enjoyed, and his inclusive teaching of purity probably did bring en-thusiastic followers into the Temple with him. But in addition, there

---

8. For a full discussion, see Chilton, *The Temple of Jesus.*

was another factor: Jesus could not simply be dispatched as a cultic criminal. He was not attempting an onslaught upon the Temple as such; his dispute with the authorities concerned purity within the Temple. Other rabbis of his period also engaged in physical demonstrations of the purity they required in the conduct of worship. One of them, for example, is said once to have driven thousands of sheep into the Temple, so that people could offer sacrifice in the manner he approved of (see Besah 20a–b in the Babylonian Talmud). Jesus' action was extreme, but not totally without precedent, even in the use of force.

The delay of the authorities, then, was understandable. We may also say it was commendable, reflecting continued controversy over the merits of Jesus' teaching and whether his occupation of the great court should be condemned out of hand. But why did they finally arrest Jesus? The last supper provides the key; something about Jesus' meals after his occupation of the Temple caused Judas to inform on Jesus. Of course, "Judas" is the only name which the traditions of the New Testament have left us. We cannot say who or how many of the disciples became disaffected by Jesus' behavior after his occupation of the Temple.

However they learned of Jesus' new interpretation of his meals of fellowship, the authorities arrested him just after the supper we call last. Jesus continued to celebrate fellowship at table as a foretaste of the kingdom, just as he had before. But he also added a new and scandalous dimension of meaning. His occupation of the Temple having failed, Jesus said of the wine, "This is my blood," and of the bread, "This is my flesh." The texts of the Synoptic Gospels, cited on the facing page, vary widely, and yet they agree on this central point both among themselves and with other early Christian literature.

However striking the variety of these texts may seem, it only grows when the others are considered (see 1 Cor. 11:24–25 and Justin, *Apology* 66.3). The reference to wine and bread as blood and flesh is the feature of agreement which makes the characteristic Christian praxis of eucharist consistent and coherent.

In Jesus' context, the context of his confrontation with the authorities of the Temple, his words can have had only one meaning. He cannot have meant, "Here are my personal body and blood;" that is an interpretation which only makes sense at a later stage. Jesus' point was rather that, in the absence of a Temple which permitted his view of purity to be practiced, wine was his blood of sacrifice, and bread was his flesh of sacrifice. In Aramaic, "blood" and "flesh" (which may also be rendered

Matthew 26:21–29

And while they were eating, he said, "Amen I say to you that one from you will deliver me over." They grieved exceedingly and began to say to him, each one, "Not I, Lord!" He replied and said, "The one who dips the hand with me in the bowl, he will deliver me over. The one like the person departs, exactly as was written about him. But miseries for that person through whom the one like the person is delivered over. Better for him if that person had not been born." Yudah, the one who delivered him over, replied and said, "Not I, Rabbi!" He says to him, "You have said." They were eating and Yeshua took bread, and blessed, broke, and giving it to the students said, "Take, eat, this is my body." He took a cup and gave thanks and gave to them, saying, "All drink from it, because this is my blood of the covenant, poured out concerning many for release of sins. But I say to you, from now I shall not drink from this yield of the vine until that day when I drink it with you new in the sovereignty of my Father."

Mark 14:18–25

And as they were reposing and eating Yeshua said, "Amen I say to you that one from you will deliver me over, the one who eats with me." They began to grieve and to say to him, one by one, "Not I!" But he said to them, "One of the twelve, who dips with me in the one bowl. For the one like the person departs, exactly as was written about him. But misery for that person through whom the one like the person is delivered over. Better for him if that person had not been born." They were eating and he took bread and blessed, broke, and gave to them and said, "Take, this is my body." He took a cup, gave thanks and gave to them, and they all drank of it. And he said to them, "This is my blood of the covenant, poured out on behalf of many. Amen I say to you, I shall no longer drink from the yield of the vine until that day when I drink it new in the sovereignty of God."

Luke 22:14–23

And when the hour came, he leaned back, and the delegates with him. [15]And he said to them, "With desire I desired to eat this Pesach with you before my suffering. [16]Because I say to you: 'I will no longer it eat until when it is fulfilled in the sovereignty of God.'" [17]He accepted a cup, gave thanks, and said, "Take this and divide among yourselves. [18]Because I say to you that I will not drink from now from the yield of the vine until when the sovereignty of God comes." [19]He took bread and gave thanks, broke, and gave to them, saying, "This is my body, given for you. Do this for my memorial." [20]And the cup similarly, after dining, saying, "This cup is the new covenant in my blood, poured out on behalf of you. Except see: the hand of the one who delivers me over is with me at the table. For the one like the person proceeds, according to what was determined. Except: miseries for that person through whom he is delivered over." [23]And they began themselves to investigate among themselves who of them, after all, was about to do this.

as "body") can carry such a sacrificial meaning, and in Jesus' context, that is the most natural meaning.

The meaning of "the last supper," then, actually evolved over a series of meals after Jesus' occupation of the Temple. During that period, Jesus claimed that wine and bread were a better sacrifice than what was offered in the Temple: at least wine and bread were Israel's own, not tokens of priestly dominance. No wonder the opposition to him, even among the Twelve (in the shape of Judas, according to the Gospels) became deadly. In essence, Jesus made his meals into a rival altar, and we may call such a reading of his words a ritual or cultic interpretation.

The cultic interpretation has two advantages over the traditional, autobiographical interpretation as the meaning Jesus attributed to his own final meals. The first advantage is contextual: the cultic interpretation places Jesus firmly with the Judaism of his period, and at the same time amply accounts for the opposition of the authorities to him. The second advantage is its explanatory power in relation to subsequent developments: the cultic interpretation enables us to explain sequentially the understandings of eucharist within earliest Christianity. The cultic sense of Jesus' last meals with his disciples is the generative meaning which permits us to explain its later meanings as eucharistic covenant, Passover, heroic symposium, and Mystery.

Six Types of Eucharistic Practice
behind "The Last Supper"

The six types of practice may be succinctly reviewed now, on the understanding that they have been developed in exegetical terms in *A Feast of Meanings,* and in religio-historical terms in *Jesus' Prayer and Jesus' Eucharist.* Jesus joined with his followers in Galilee and Judaea, both disciples and sympathizers, in meals which were designed to anticipate the coming of God's kingdom. The meals were characterized by a readiness to accept the hospitality and the produce of Israel at large. A willingness to provide for the meals, to join in the fellowship, to forgive and to be forgiven, was seen by Jesus as a sufficient condition for eating in his company and for entry into the kingdom.

Jesus' view of purity was distinctive, and — no doubt — lax in the estimation of many contemporary rabbis. In one regard, however, he typifies the Judaism of his period: there was an evident fit between his practice of fellowship at meals and his theory of what was clean. Meals appear to have been a primary marker of social grouping within the first century in Palestine. Commensal institutions, formal or not, were plentiful. They included the banquets of Qumran, but also occasions of local or national festivity throughout the country. Any patron who mounted a banquet would appropriately expect the meal to reflect his or her views of purity, and guests would not be in a good position to militate in favor of other views. But meals need not be on a grand scale to be seen as important, and much more modest events might be subject to custom: a house-hold might welcome a feast or shabbath with a cup of sanctification (the *kiddush*), and bless bread as a prelude to a significant family affair (the *be-rakhah*). In addition, collegial meals shared within fellowships (*haburoth*) at which like-minded fellows (*haberim*) would share the foods and the company they considered pure would define distinct social groups.

Jesus' practice coincided to some extent with that of a *haburah*, but his construal of purity was unusual. Given the prominence accorded wine in his meals and the way his characteristic prayer emphasizes the theme of sanctification, we might describe the first type of his meals — the practice of purity in anticipation of the kingdom — as a *kiddush* of the kingdom. But his meals were not limited to households, so that there is already, in its simplest form, a metaphorical quality about this practice. Any analogy with the communal meals of Qumran would seem to be strained, unless the feedings of the five thousand (Matt. 14:13–21; Mark 6:32–44; Luke 9:10–17) and the four thousand (Matt. 15:32–38; Mark 8:1–9) are held originally to have been staged as massive banquets designed to instance Jesus' theory of purity and his expectation of the kingdom.

Indeed, there is practically no meal of Judaism with which Jesus' meals do not offer some sort of analogy, because the meal was a seal and an occasion of purity, and Jesus was concerned with what was pure. But both the nature of his concern and the character of his meals were distinctive in their inclusiveness: Israel as forgiven and willing to provide of its own produce was for him the occasion of the kingdom. That was the first type in the development of the eucharist.

Jesus himself brought about the final crisis of his career. His teaching in regard to the kingdom and its purity, including his communal meals as enacted parables, might have been continued indefinitely (for all the controversy involved) outside of Jerusalem. But he sought to influence practice in the Temple, where the purity of Israel was supremely instanced and where the feast of all nations promised by the prophets was to occur. A dispute over the location of vendors of animals for sacrifice was the catalyst in a raging dispute over purity between Jesus (with his followers) and the authorities in the Temple.

The riot in the Temple which Jesus provoked may have been sufficient by itself to bring about his execution, given the importance of
the Temple within both Judaism and the settlement with Rome. But he
compounded his confrontation with the authorities by putting a new interpretation upon the meals people took with him in their expectation of
the kingdom. As he shared wine, he referred to it as the equivalent of the
blood of an animal, shed in sacrifice; when he shared bread, he claimed
its value was as that of sacrificial flesh. Such offerings were purer, more
readily accepted by God, than what was sacrificed in a Temple which had
become corrupt. Here was a sacrifice of sharings which the authorities
could not control, and which the nature of Jesus' movement made it
impossible for them to ignore. Jesus' meals after his failed occupation of
the Temple became a surrogate of sacrifice, the second type of eucharist.

The third type is that of Petrine Christianity, when the blessing or
breaking of bread at home, the *berakhah* of Judaism, became a principal model of eucharist. A practical result of that development was that
bread came to have precedence over wine. More profoundly, the circle of
Peter conceived of Jesus as a new Moses (see especially the narrative of
Jesus' Transfiguration, Matt. 17:1–8; Mark 9:2–10; Luke 9:28–36), who
gave commands concerning purity as Moses did on Sinai, and who also
expected his followers to worship on Mount Zion. As compared to Jesus'
practice (in its first and second stages), Petrine practice represents a double domestication. First, adherents of the movement congregated in the
homes of their colleagues, rather than seeking the hospitality of others.
Second, the validity of sacrifice in the Temple was acknowledged. Both
forms of domestication — clearly attested in the book of Acts (see 2:42–
47) — grew out of the new circumstances of the movement in Jerusalem
and fresh opportunities for worship in the Temple; they changed the nature of the meal and the memory of what Jesus had said at the "last
supper." The application of the model of a *berakhah* to eucharist was
a self-conscious metaphor, because the careful identification of those
gathered in Jesus' name with a household was itself metaphorical.

The fourth type of eucharist, the contribution of the circle of James,
pursued the tendency of domestication further. The eucharist was seen
as a Seder, in terms of both its meaning and its chronology. That identification was accomplished in two of the Synoptic Gospels by framing the
"last supper" within a description of preparations for Passover that has
no connection with the eucharistic narrative itself (see Matt. 26:6–13;
Mark 14:3–9). That, together with the fact that Luke and John do not
present the "last supper" as a Seder, indicates the artificiality of the tra-

dition. So understood, only circumcised Jews in a state of purity could participate in eucharist (so Exod. 12:48), which could be truly recollected only once a year, at Passover in Jerusalem. The Quartodeciman controversy (concerning the timing of Easter) of a later period, fierce though it appears, was but a shadow cast by a much more serious contention concerning the nature of Christianity. The Jacobean program was to integrate Jesus' movement fully within the liturgical institutions of Judaism, to insist upon the Judaic identity of the movement and upon Jerusalem as its governing center. Nonetheless, there is never any doubt but that eucharist is not portrayed as an actual replacement of the Seder of Israel as such, and for that reason the language of metaphor is appropriate here, as well.

Paul and the Synoptic Gospels represent the fifth type of eucharist. Paul vehemently resists Jacobean claims, by insisting Jesus' last meal occurred on the night in which he was betrayed (1 Cor. 11:23), not on Passover. He emphasizes the link between Jesus' death and the eucharist, and he accepts the Hellenistic refinement of the Petrine type which presented the eucharist as a sacrifice for sin (1 Cor. 11:24). That type is also embraced in the Synoptic Gospels, where the heroism of Jesus is such that the meal is an occasion to join in the solidarity of martyrdom. The Synoptic strategy is not to oppose the Jacobean program directly; in fact, the Passover chronology is accepted (although not without internal contradiction). Instead, the Synoptics insist by various wordings that Jesus' blood is shed in the interests of the communities for which those Gospels were composed, for the "many" in Damascus (Matt. 26:28) and Rome (Mark 14:24), on behalf of "you" in Antioch (Luke 22:20). The Synoptic tradition also provided two stories of miraculous feeding which symbolized the inclusion of Jews and non-Jews within eucharist, understood as in the nature of a philosophical symposium (see Mark 6:32–44; 8:1–19 and parallels). This willingness to explore differing meanings with eucharistic action attests that any such meaning, taken singly, was understood metaphorically.

The feeding of the five thousand — understood as occurring at Passover — is taken up in John 6 in a fully Paschal sense. Jesus himself is identified as the manna, miraculous food bestowed by God upon his people. The motif was already articulated by Paul (1 Cor. 10:1–4), but John develops it to construe the eucharist as a Mystery, in which Jesus offers his own flesh and blood (carefully defined to avoid a crude misunderstanding; John 6:30–34, 41–58). That autobiographical reading of Jesus' words — as giving his personal body and blood in eucharist —

had already occurred to Hellenistic Christians who followed Synoptic practice. The Johannine practice made that meaning as explicit as
the break with Judaism is in the fourth Gospel. Both that departure
and the identification of Jesus himself (rather than his supper) as the
Paschal lamb are pursued in the Revelation (5:6–14; 7:13–17). The sixth
type of eucharist can only be understood as a consciously non-Judaic
and Hellenistic development. It involves participants in joining by oath
(*sacramentum* in Latin, corresponding to *musterion* within the Greek vocabulary of primitive Christianity) in the sacrifice of the Mysterious hero
himself, separating themselves from others. Eucharist has become sacra-
ment, and involves a knowing conflict with the ordinary understanding
of what Judaism might and might not include.

"The Last Supper" is neither simply Jesus' Seder nor simply a symposium of Hellenists to which the name of Jesus happens to have been
attached. Such ideological regimens, which will have the Gospels be only
historical or only fictive, simply starve the reader of the meanings which
generated the texts to hand. The engines of those meanings were diverse
practices, whose discovery permits us to feast on the richness of traditional praxis. A generative exegesis of eucharistic texts may not conclude
with a single meaning which is alleged to have occasioned all the others.
One of the principal findings of such an approach is rather that meaning itself is to some extent epiphenomenal, a consequence of a definable
practice with its own initial sense being introduced into a fresh environment of people who in turn take up the practice as they understand
it and produce their own meanings. The sense with which a practice is
mediated to a community is therefore one measure of what that community will finally produce as its practice, but the initial meaning does
not determine the final meaning.

The meanings conveyed by words must be the point of departure for a
generative exegesis, because those meanings are our only access to what
produced the texts to hand. But having gained that access, it becomes
evident that eucharist is not a matter of the development of a single,
basic meaning within several different environments. Those environments have themselves produced various meanings under the influence
of definable practices. Eucharist was not simply handed on as a tradition.
Eucharistic traditions were rather the catalyst which permitted communities to crystallize their own practice in oral or textual form. What they
crystallized was a function of the practice which had been learned, palpable gestures with specified objects and previous meanings, along with the
meaning and the emotional response which the community discovered

in eucharist. There is no history of the tradition apart from a history of meaning, a history of emotional response, a history of practice: the practical result of a generative exegesis of eucharistic texts is that practice itself is an appropriate focus in understanding the New Testament.

The Moment of Magical Surrogacy

If Jesus is seen as generating eucharist as a surrogate of sacrifice, the question emerges: how can he have undertaken such an action, with such an understanding? In terms of circumstance, his failed occupation of the Temple provides an adequate occasion, but not a sufficient cause from the point of view of his motivation.

Some years ago, I taught a course to my students at Bard College with a professor of Asian religions.[9] Our purpose was to read through the group of theorists whose work has been formative of the discipline of the study of religion in the United States, including William Robertson Smith, James George Frazer, Emile Durkheim, Max Weber, Bronislaw Malinowski, Marcel Mauss, Victor Turner, Edward Evan Evans-Pritchard, Clifford Geertz, René Girard, and Catherine Bell. The point of focus we selected was magic, and I came to realize, particularly through our reading of Max Weber, that the myth of the magician as originator might be clouding our perception of that category.

Ralph Schroeder has made an especially interesting contribution from this point of view.[10] Despite the criticism of Weber as an "intellectualist," Schroeder is attracted by Weber's linkage of magic, religion, and science: "In Weber's view, magic has a rational aim which is pursued by irrational means, whereas religion is characterized by an increasingly irrational aim and increasingly rational means to salvation."[11] Schroeder continues:

> The most undifferentiated form of magic, in Weber's view, is where magical power is thought to be embodied in a person who can bring about supernatural events by virtue of an innate capacity. This belief is the original source of charisma. 'The oldest of all "callings" or professions,' Weber points out, 'is that of the magician' (1981a:8). From this point, charisma develops by a process of abstraction to-

---

9. My former colleague, Laurie Patton, is now pursing this interest in a study of mantra in domestic religious practices in early India.

10. *Max Weber and the Sociology of Culture* (London: Sage, 1992) 33–71, a chapter entitled "The Uniqueness of the East."

11. *Max Weber and the Sociology of Culture*, 34.

wards the notion that certain forces are 'behind' this extraordinary power — although they remain within the world (1968: 401).[12]

This leads to an analysis of magic as static:

> The inflexibility of the means employed with magic creates a static system of norms and ritual prescriptions which reinforces traditional conduct. Charisma, inasmuch as it is tied to concrete embodiments and tangible successes, easily becomes routinized. Moreover, the unchallengeable position of the magicians consti-tutes an obstacle to cultural change because by attaching sacred norms to economic, political, and other functions, the magician sanctions their traditional role as well.[13]

This contrasts sharply with the dynamic quality of religion:

> That is, the world as a whole must have a meaning outside of what is empirically given. It should be emphasized that this a feature of all the great religions — again, Weber refers to them as *Kulturreligionen* (1980b: 367). This is notable because here we have what is, from the viewpoint of a sociology of culture, an answer to Weber's lack of a concept of 'society': the unity that this concept affords else-where is here taken on by the unity of 'culture' in the form of the *Kulturreligionen*.[14]

What Schroeder does not say, and yet may easily be inferred from his study, is that magic should not be seen as the foundation of religion, but as a specific manifestation of religion, when the entire system is held to be concentrated in an individual or individuals. Magic expresses more the crisis of a system than the presupposition of a system.

Such a description accords rather well with some of the figures whom Josephus calls "false prophets." There has been a tendency to class John the baptist with them, whose followers presumably called them prophets. In fact, Josephus simply calls John a good man (*Antiquities* 18 §117), and describes Bannus' similar commitment to sanctification by bathing in approving terms (*Life* §11). Nothing they did (as related by Josephus) can be compared with what Josephus said the false prophets did: one scaled Mount Gerizim to find the vessels deposited by Moses (*Antiquities*

---

12. *Max Weber and the Sociology of Culture*, 37, citing *Wirtschaftsgeschichte* (Berlin: Duncker and Humblot, 1981) and *Economy and Society* (New York: Bedminster, 1968).
13. *Max Weber and the Sociology of Culture*, 38–9.
14. *Max Weber and the Sociology of Culture*, 40, citing *Wirtschaft und Gesellschaft* (Tübingen: Mohr, 1980).

18 §§85–87), Theudas waited at the Jordan for the waters to part for him, as they had for Joshua (*Antiquities* 20 §§97–98),[15] the Egyptian marched from the Mount of Olives in the hope the walls of Jerusalem might fall at his command (*Antiquities* 20 §§169–172) so that he might conquer Jerusalem (*War* 2 §261–263). If there is an act in the Gospels which approximates to such fanaticism, it is Jesus' entry into Jerusalem and his occupation of the Temple; apparently he expected to prevail against all the odds in insisting upon his own understanding of what true purity there was, in opposition to Caiaphas and the imposing authority of a high priest sanctioned by Rome. When Jesus is styled a prophet in Matt. 21:11, 46, that may have something to do with the usage of Josephus, but to portray John the baptist in such terms is incautious.

These acts of magic are not spontaneous or heroic foundations of new religions by means of Weberian charisma. Rather, each instantiates a response to a sense of crisis, the conviction that the entire religious system has gone wrong, and may only be retrieved by a magician who takes that system on to himself. Finding Moses' vessels, parting the Jordan, taking Jerusalem, and occupying the Temple are all examples of the attempt to right the system by seizing and manipulating its most central symbols. They are instances of magic as theurgy, the access of divine power in order to change and mold the ordinary structures of authority, whether social or natural.[16]

It is in this context that I find Bernhard Lang's work as intriguing as I do. I must admit that, when he first suggested precise connections between Jesus' last meals and normally sacrificial acts,[17] I reacted with some reserve. Now, however, he has specified those connections in great detail, and — at the same time — the sense of such connections is clearer to me. In taking the Temple to his table, Jesus not only celebrated God's sovereignty and marked that celebration as an acceptable sacrifice; he

---

15. According to Colin Brown, Theudas was inspired by John the baptist, whose program was not purification but a recrossing of the Jordan; see "What Was John the Baptist Doing?" *Bulletin for Biblical Research* 7 (1997) 37–49, 48. That seems a desperate expedient to avoid John's obvious connection with purification. The equally obvious obstacles are that crossing the Jordan is not a part of any characterization of John's message in the primary sources, and that Josephus does not associate John with the "false prophets." For the context of John's immersion (and Jesus'), see Chilton, *Jesus' Baptism and Jesus' Healing: His Personal Practice of Spirituality* (Harrisburg: Trinity Press International, 1998).

16. Such is the sense of magic which stands behind the works of Morton Smith, *The Secret Gospel* (New York; Harper and Row, 1973) and *Jesus the Magician* (New York: Harper and Row, 1977). Throughout, what is apparent is the influence of Hans Lewy, *Chaldean Oracles and Theurgy* (Cairo: Institut français d'archéologie orientale, 1956).

17. See his article in *Bible Review* 10.6 (December 1994).

also marked that magical surrogacy as the means of the fulfillment of Israel.

Eucharistic practice, especially at the Synoptic level, marks the realization of that magical surrogacy within the community of believers. Jesus' giving of himself within the meal is indeed a heroic act of martyrdom, after the pattern of the Maccabean martyrs, but it is also an occasion of the characteristically Christian double mimesis to which we have referred. By the community's repetition of his action, Jesus conveys the divine pleasure in accepting the celebration of God's sovereignty as sacrifice. That means there is an entire dimension of meaning outside the sphere of what is usually called "heroic," or even a martyr's witness, because the action involved is God's extension into the community by means of Jesus, not simply a demonstration of Jesus' courage. At the same time, the Synoptic Gospels in their differing ways weave the experience of believers into the sacrifice of Jesus, so that their own potential martyrdom — a practical possibility within the social world of the New Testament as a whole — is made a seal of their genuine participation in the eucharist. Christianity made its martyrs out of the recognition that it takes no special heroism to die, but that a faithful death extends the reach of Christ's own sacrifice, both in the direction from God to humanity and in the dimension from humanity to God.

"Amen, Amen, I say to you, unless you eat the flesh of the son of man and drink his blood, you do not have life in yourselves" (John 6:53). As we have already seen above, these words mark a conscious departure from Judaism, along the lines of a theology of the Mysteries. But the increasingly Hellenistic complexion of the Johannine community in Ephesus (around 100 C.E.) did not alone necessitate this departure. Rather, the language of Mystery is here used in order to express the logic of mimesis as it had been discovered during the seventy-some years of eucharistic praxis prior to the composition of John's Gospel.

Jesus' designation of himself as "the bread of life" in the Johannine discourse which immediately precedes provides the grounding logic of this incorporation of Jesus' mimesis within oneself (John 6:48–51):

> I am the bread of life. Your fathers ate the Manna in the wilderness and died. This is the bread that descends from heaven, so that anyone might eat from it and not die. I am the living bread that descends from heaven; if anyone eats from this bread, one will live forever, and the bread which I will give is also my flesh, on behalf of the life of the world.

The double metaphor — bread as life, bread as flesh — typifies the Johannine mastery of poetic expression: vocabulary and syntax are scarified to the point of simplicity, so as to point to the complexity of the metaphorical design. In this case, the Johannine poem designs the eucharistic bread as that which provides eternal life and, at one and the same time, involves historical death. That martyrdom of Jesus, uniquely related to the self-giving love of God, is ingested in eucharist, so as to become the vocation of every Christian, begotten from God and knowing God by pursuing God's love (1 John 4:7).

SEVEN

Conclusion

The analysis of our texts, introduced in the Preface, as addressing issues commonly elicited within the field of spirituality teaches us both about those texts and about the makeup of spirituality itself. The texts themselves speak in relation to the entire system of religion which generated them, so there can be no genuinely critical reading, no meaningful exegesis, apart from the awareness of how documents frame their meanings within their theological and historical environments. The apparent simplicity of this principle — and its self-evidence, when one starts from the perspective of the critical study of religion — has not permitted it to be widely applied within academic circles. Indeed, perhaps its simplicity explains why it has eluded the design of most curricula in higher education. But alongside the simple exegetical principle we have encountered, we have also had to deal with a complexity that has been obscured in contemporary discussion. It is a truism among popular writers that, while the study of religion and theology is complicated, spirituality is a straightforward matter of being "in touch" with the divine, much as one might be "in touch" with one's feelings. As we have explored what it means to approach the center of one's religion, the fact of one's own death, and the challenge of exemplary martyrdom, it has become quite plain that Judaism and Christianity both engage the affective life, but also that what one can be "in touch" with or feel is in no sense the limit of what they have to teach us. Hence our second principle, uncovered by our discussion: It belongs to the character of a genuine spirituality that it includes *and* transcends personal feeling. Both these principles are revolutionary in their implications for how we study and practice religion, and we need to explain some of the implications of each in turn.

First, the challenge to the academic study of religion and theology, which is in any case the easier challenge to explain and illustrate. A letter was addressed to one of us, very much like many such letters, asking for permission to reproduce an article. The letter came from the Computing

Services of Oxford University, and asked authorization to include a piece within what is evidently a very sensible scheme in technical terms:[1]

> This small-scale project will make pages from selected texts available in digital format to students studying one paper of the first-year undergraduate degree. The scheme will use the University's network facilities to make the texts available within Oxford University and not more widely. The texts will be distributed as electro-images rather than "full text," thus eliminating the risk of errors being introduced into the text. The project is a non-profit venture and is being run for purely educational purposes.

In its address of the problem of corruption within electronic resources, as well as in its design for the use of the students, the project is well designed and innovative — in that regard, a model of what might be attempted elsewhere.

But innovation in the use of electronic resources all too often masks a staid, counterproductive conservatism in regard to curricular substance. The letter goes on:

> The Introduction to *The Kingdom of God in the Teaching of Jesus* (1984) published by SPCK and Fortress Press has been selected by the academic staff as core reading for the undergraduates taking the *Mark* paper. We would very much like to include the introductory section in the collection of texts which are made available to students, if you are willing to grant us permission.

Examinations in Theology at Oxford follow the European model, in organizing the curriculum of each final examination ("paper," in the jargon) at the close of the three-year course (and after the first year) to accommodate the analysis of particular books of the Old and New Testaments. This exegetical focus, document by document, is an inheritance of the nineteenth century, especially under the influence of Brooke Foss Westcott at Cambridge and William Sanday at Oxford.

In its time, this documentary emphasis was revolutionary and productive. It freed the students and fellows of colleges at Cambridge and Oxford from the necessity of adhering to a doctrinal reading of Scripture (which the statutes of those universities had formally demanded), so that critical reflection became possible. But now, a century after that revolution, documentary reading has itself become doctrinaire. So, for example, in the

---

1. The letter, dated July 6, 1999, was written by Ms. Sarah Porter.

examinations at Oxford (typical of many others in Europe), *Mark* is used to define a field of reflection, as if were a self-contained, literary unit. Then, so many such units provide for the discipline of the study of the New Testament within Theology. This atomism in the approach to the Scriptures is enshrined in the theological curricula of most European universities to this day, and it is largely replicated in American seminaries and schools of divinity, which have not so far proven to be creative institutions.

American universities, by contrast, have prided themselves in providing courses and majors in what is often styled comparative religion, offered on an anthropological basis. To make the distinction from anthropology, offerings in religion are frequently styled as "cultural studies," or "studies in the theory of culture." They are devoted to the theoretical study of particular religions, usually without reference (or with only scant reference) to the texts which those religions themselves designate as foundational. Periodically, departments of religion or theology are riven with disputes between comparativists and exegetes, and careers are made and unmade on the basis of a distinction between two equally untenable positions.

Because a text such as the Gospel according to Mark was generated within primitive Christianity as a composite, communal effort, the document *in its own literary terms of reference* cannot reasonably be isolated from its contemporaneous environment. In that environment, what we would call Christianity was on the cusp of Judaism and the independent religion it was to become: the character of *Mark* is violated when it is read as an independent, literary exercise by an author who could treat his materials freely according to his own will. Fixation on the limits of a document, whether in the New Testament or in Mishnah and Talmud, can only lead to a distorted, pedantic version of what the document means to say. Equally, the Christianity which is the environment of Mark and the other Gospels, the Judaism of Mishnah and Talmud, cannot be appreciated simply on the basis of received generalizations concerning the content of Christian or Judaic faith. The cultural or comparative study of religion cannot be served by the alleged "observation" of a given group (ancient or modern), as if in the production of an ethnography, because the observer brings with her or him the very categories of what it means to be Christian or Jewish which are under study. An exegesis or a theory which is not grounded in the self-expression of the religion at issue indulges in the projection of the self and the repetition of stereotypes.

Our response to the atomism of the one-sidedly exegetical European model and to the generality of the one-sidedly theoretical American model is to focus on the perspectives which religions themselves produce under the scrutiny of a generative exegesis. If a system of religion has gone to the trouble of articulating itself self-consciously by means of text, we argue, that becomes an opportunity to free ourselves from the rigidity involved in treating every text as if it were one author's exercise or as if it were the epitome of the beliefs we now use to identify Judaism and Christianity. Briefly put: the rabbis of the dual Torah were not motivated by a desire to found "Rabbinic Judaism," but to articulate the will and the pleasure of the Holy One, Blessed be He, and the apostolic tradition was not intended from the outset to make Christianity a separate religion from Judaism, but to realize the unity of the human impulse towards God and the divine movement towards humanity by means of the cross. But both, the dual Torah and the apostolic tradition, owe their significance to the beliefs and practices which developed in their wake. So — if we would read them critically — we need to read them with careful attention to their peculiarities in the generative fashion which brings us from their originating contexts to the environments they themselves helped to produce. That is just the generative exegesis, with the appropriate regard to historical circumstance and setting, which has informed the present volume. Insofar as our approach is influential within academic circles, both atomism and generality will give way to a textually focused but systemic reading of Scripture in the future, in which an eye to detail does not exclude a view to perspective, and in which a concern for cultural meaning is not reduced to solipsism.[2]

The second principle we have encountered is not simply of academic interest. Spirituality has become one of the most widely discussed areas within popular philosophy, especially in the United States, but increasingly in Europe. Our selection of topics — knowing God, dying in good faith, and bearing faithful witness to God through martyrdom — has been guided by the prevalent reference to all three in this type of discussion. Commonly, these topics are taken to be typical of human experience, because the call to encounter God, the fact of our mortality, and the glory of religious heroism all seem embedded in human experience.

But it is the very characterization of the topics as "experience" that is called radically into question by our analysis. Each has been addressed, as promised, on the basis of the classic or canonical writings of Judaism and Christianity, and although the topics are stable as one moves from one

---

2. At Bard College, our procedure has been to see to the placement of exegetes in the professoriate, with each of the global religions (Buddhism, Christianity, Hinduism, Islam, Judaism) represented. Students, then, are exposed to each of those religions, and are encouraged to learn a primary exegetical language of the religion that interests them most.

religion to the other, what has been said in respect of each has proven to be oddly and strikingly incommensurate. If we look back at what has been said, topic by topic, it becomes apparent that the comparison of these two religions is not simply a matter of tracing topical agreement and disagreement, but also involves accounting for profoundly differing conceptions of what it means to know God, to die, to be a martyr. All three, it turns out, are not common experiences, but points of intersection between these two religions (and other perspectives not traced here), each of them viewing those points from a distinctive angle.

The Judaist typified by our sources encounters the Torah with an all-consuming honesty, founded on the conviction that, in intellectual interaction "we are held together in our argument by shared conviction that what is at stake is truth, not power, nor personalities, nor even the merely formal rituals of an empty academicism such as we may see acted out on an academic stage here or there" (above, p. 22). The life of the mind, collectively cultivated, features as the central instrument of the "experience" of God. The pivot of Christian spirituality, by contrast, is that Jesus' "*kabbalah* offers the vision of God in his glory because divine Spirit makes that vision possible" (p. 44). Dedicated to visionary discipline as the central instrument of its "experience" of God, Christianity privileges an emotional attachment to Jesus over an intellectual apprehension of Jesus, God, or *any* theological topic.

Precisely in the comparison of how Judaism and Christianity approach the issue of access to God, we can understand how people of the one religion can stereotype people of the other religion in the ways that they typically have. For those whose access to God is communal and intellectual, a matter of argument, Christianity must appear to be ill defined and sentimental. And for those who access is emotional and visionary, a matter of personal attachment, Judaism will inevitably be characterized as abstract and legalist. Much well-intentioned effort has gone into dispelling such stereotypes; we suggest they are persistent because there is a grain of truth in them.

The problem with these stereotypes resides not in what they say, but in what they fail to go on to say. They treat Judaism as if it were a religion of the head, and Christianity a religion of the heart. But all the great religious systems of the world, Judaism and Christianity as well as Buddhism, Hinduism, and Islam, are religions of head and heart and hands. Their capacity to form cultures and then to reform them, powerfully and persistently, stems from their combination of human intellect, human affect, and human practice within comprehensive and evolving traditions of how people are to think, feel, and act.[3] For just that reason, religions may be analyzed and compared according to the world view they articulate (their intellectual paradigm), their view of the social order (which models the affections of the community), and the way of life they espouse (as the praxis appropriate to humanity).[4]

So, in the present volume, Christianity shows itself fully prepared to deploy an exacting intellectual analysis when it concerns, not the issue of access to God, but the significance of human death. Rather than approaching that as a irreducible fact of our mortality, Christians see it as "a profound shift in the very medium in which we are human" (p. 91), such that the prospect of spiritual being is opened up for us. Judaists (and, indeed, the majority of non-Christians) are likely to see that as fanciful, a denial of an obvious condition of life, while Christians' attachment to the conviction that the Spirit of God has entered our life in Jesus commits them to *analyzing* death, rather than merely mourning it. In sharp contrast, "within the spirituality of Judaism, death is a homecoming" (p. 67), rather than a transformation, because — whether or not resurrection is at issue — death represents the supreme moment of humility before the Torah which the sage is committed to during his entire life. Judaism confronts death with the persistent practice of the same virtues it endorses every day, confronting the fact of mortality with its own way of life. At just the moment the Christian becomes intellectual, the Judaist remains practical.

Finally, martyrdom. Here we encounter our biggest surprise. In reaction against the heroic portrayal of Jesus' death as a martyr, it is widely asserted that Judaism lays no emphasis on the concept of martyrdom. From the sources, we have now seen otherwise: "The martyr stands for the entirety of Israel's history, the martyr's ultimate destiny, Israel's divinely planned reward: to live forever" (p. 112). In historical terms, that helps us to explain the emergence of Christianity, with its systemic focus on Jesus, but the religious significance of this fact is even greater than its historical significance. As Judaism's head is occupied with the Torah, and its hands with the praxis the Torah prescribes or implies, so its heart

---

3. For an analysis of how religions develop in mimetic terms in their coordination of intellect, affect, and praxis, see Chilton, *The Temple of Jesus. His Sacrificial Program Within a Cultural History of Sacrifice* (University Park: The Pennsylvania State University Press, 1992). As that work makes plain, no limitation to the global religions is implied by the analysis; indeed, I would argue that religion in its proper sense is to be defined as the nexus of those three features of human consciousness as they are articulated within a social sphere of any kind and of any size.

4. See Neusner, *Judaism without Christianity. An Introduction to the Religious System of the Mishnah in Historical Context* (Hoboken: Ktav, 1991).

is filled with a passionate affection for humble obedience as the fundamental and most beautiful virtue. And just here, where one might expect
the hearty agreement of Christianity, there is a bewildering anticlimax.
Martyrdom becomes a matter of how you live your life and eat your
bread: the "martyrdom of Jesus, uniquely related to the self-giving love
of God, is ingested in eucharist, so as to become the vocation of every
Christian, begotten from God and knowing God by pursuing God's love"
(p. 131). The topic of martyrdom shows up the Judaist at one's most
affective, the Christian at one's most practical.

Just as the terms "Judaist" and "Christian" here are typological, rather
than normative, so the distinctions we have made among the intellectual, the affective, and the practical are obviously not intended to be
hard and fast. Each interpenetrates the other, and yet the emphasis on
one sort of consciousness, with the relative backgrounding of the other
two, is evident, important, and influential. Indeed, that emphasis is so
influential, it produces different constructions of what it means to engage with one's God, to die, to suffer as a martyr. These "experiences,"
it turns out, are actually not common at all; each is distinctive, according to the religious system within which it is produced. But at the same
time, Judaism and Christianity can become intelligible to one another,
if they relate *both* intersecting topics to one another, *and* the systemic
instruments of consciousness which those topics engage.

Spirituality, then, is more than the sum of what a person might report of the experience of God and related topics; rather, it involves the
composition of experience itself within the religious system which makes
a culture and a consciousness possible. For that reason, the systematic
comparison of religions is a necessary condition for the understanding of
any spirituality. The distinctive qualities of Judaism and Christianity only
become apparent under comparison; without it, the spirituality of each
seems just to be a matter of a relatively greater or lesser degree of piety.
In fact, what the spiritualities of both religions effect is a characteristic
archetype of how people meet God, face death, and learn transcendence
while they are dying.

This volume represents something of the possibility both religions offer
of learning transcendence while we are alive. When we understand each
as a system, and permit them to relate to one another by means of
recognizable topics, theologically pertinent to both, the result is that we
see, not only how and why the religions are different, but what their
characteristic spiritualities consist of. And in learning that, we see how
our world, how our experience, is made.

Index